Nita Mehta's
Low Calorie
cooking for the Indian kitchen

Nita Mehta

M.Sc. (Food and Nutrition), Gold Medalist

SNAB
Publishers Pvt. Ltd.

Nita Mehta's

Low Calorie
cooking for the Indian kitchen

© Copyright 2001-2003 SNAB Publishers Pvt Ltd

Reprint 2003

ISBN 81-7869-000-4

Food Styling & Photography: SNAB

Layout and laser typesetting:

National Information Technology Academy
3A/3, Asaf Ali Road
New Delhi-110002
☎ 3252948

Published by:

Publishers Pvt Ltd
3A/3 Asaf Ali Road
New Delhi-110002

Editorial and Marketing office:
E-348, Greater Kailash-II, N.Delhi-48
Fax: 91-11-6235218 *Tel:* 91-11-6214011, 6238727
E-Mail: nitamehta@email.com
snab@snabindia.com

The Best of Cookery Books *Website:* http://www.nitamehta.com
Website: http://www.snabindia.com

Printed at:
THOMSON PRESS (INDIA) LIMITED

Distributed by:
THE VARIETY BOOK DEPOT
A.V.G. Bhavan, M 3 Con Circus
New Delhi - 110 001
Tel: 3327175, 3322567; Fax: 3714335

Price: Rs.189/-

Introduction

*E*njoy deliciously flavoured food without feeling guilty, by cutting down on calories, yet not on taste! To get rid of that extra roll of fat, go on a low calorie diet, which includes very little or absolutely no oil. Cook oil free curries by steaming the onion masala in a pressure cooker instead of the regular way of bhuno-ing (stir frying) it in oil till cooked. Oil free, yet delicious curries can now be cooked without a fuss!

The secret of cooking delicious low fat dishes is learning how to alter ingredients. Trim fat by substituting ingredients like skimmed milk for cream and use low fat yogurt as a substitute for mayonnaise to prepare dips and sauces. For Thai or South Indian Dishes, prepare coconut milk by using desiccated coconut instead of fresh coconut, since the dry coconut powder hardly has any fat in it. I have used skimmed or toned milk wherever milk was required. Even paneer and yogurt used in the recipes should be prepared from toned or skimmed milk, instead of buying ready made paneer which is prepared from whole or full cream milk.

Be innovative. Use different sauces, herbs and spices to make the food flavourful so that you do not feel the absence of oil or butter in the dish. *Choosing* the right spice, adding the *right amount* of spice and also adding the spice at the *right time* while cooking, matters a lot. Adding a dash of mustard paste or soya sauce or a few crushed black peppercorns enhances the taste of the food immensely.

Besides all this, try using vegetables and fruits with a high fibre and water content, like water melons, peaches, papayas, spinach, mushrooms, cabbage, cucumbers, brinjals etc. Another myth that potatoes are fattening is proved wrong by cooking potatoes with very little or no oil at all. Potatoes are complex carbohydrates which keep you feeling full for long and help you to avoid snacking in between meals. Unless fried or wrongly cooked (with a lot of butter or cheese), they are an ideal food.

The book features a vast array of adventurous, nourishing and imaginative low calorie meals, including soups, salads, main dishes of Indian, Continental, Thai and Chinese origin and some low calorie desserts - all adapted to suit the Indian palate. It includes a host of mouth watering and festive recipes for all occasions, cooked the right way, for enjoying a healthier tomorrow!

Nita Mehta

To my dear daughter
Bhavna
and adorable son-in-law
Vivek
with all my love

THE DIET PYRAMID

Eat Least

Sugar, Butter, Ghee,
Margarine, Oil

Eat Proteins Moderately

Pulses, Lentils, Legumes (Dals,
Channas, Rajmah,Peas etc.)
Nuts, Milk, Cheese, Dahi

Eat Non Veg Food Moderately

Chicken, Mutton, Fish

Eat Lots

Fresh Fruits &
Vegetables

Eat Most

Bread, Cereals
(Roti)

Contents

The Diet Pyramid   7
Calorie Guidance   11

LOW CALORIE INDIAN RECIPES   13

CURRIES & WET DISHES

VEGETARIAN

Paneer Dakshin Style   14
Gatte ki Subzi   15
Rajasthani Bharwan Mirch   16
Dal Makhani   17
Oil free Matar Paneer   17
Dapka Kadhi   20
Anaarkali Aloo   24
Handi Channas without Oil   25
Quick Unfried Dahivada   26

NON-VEGETARIAN

Fish Creole   18
Kashmiri Chicken Yakhni   21
Khatti Machli   22
Chicken in Tomato Gravy   22
Chicken Malgoba Curry   23
Red Dhania Chicken   23

DRY & SEMI DRY DISHES

VEGETARIAN

Avial   28
Dahi Masala Mushrooms   31
Baked Baingan ka Bharta   31
Palak Makai Ki Subzi   33
Vegetable Jalfrazie   34
Matar Dhania Wale   34
Kesari Dahi Waale Aloo 36
Saunf Waale Khatte Baingan   38

NON-VEGETARIAN

Kadhai Chicken   30
Palak-Methi Chicken   32
Kashmiri Danival Chicken Korma   35
Elaichi Murg   35
Sukha Dahi Murg   37
Murg Kali Mirch   37

LOW FAT DISHES FROM FAR & WIDE   40

VEGETARIAN

Szechwan Baby Corns (Chinese)   41
Hot & Sour Cabbage (Chinese)   43
Spicy Honeyed Veggies (Chinese)   45
Thai Green Curry with
Paneer & Aubergines   47

NON-VEGETARIAN

Chicken Sizzler   42
Stroganoff Chicken (Continental)   44
Mediterranean Chicken   44
Quick Chilli Chicken (Chinese)   46
Thai Fish Curry   48

Basil & Tomato Pasta (Italian)　50
Bean Burritos (Mexican)　51
Vegetables in Red Curry (Thai)　52

Chicken in Red Curry (Thai)　52
Chicken Fiesta (Italian)　53
Chicken Steak (Continental)　54

FROM THE OVEN　55

BAKED, TANDOORI, GRILLED

VEGETARIAN

Tandoori Paneer with Capsicum　56
Mixed Greens Baked with Corn　57
Layered Masala Paneer　60
Ajwaini Mushrooms in
Tomato Cups　62
Red-Green-White Casserole　63
Tandoori Bharwaan Aloo　66
Tandoori Platter　68
Broccoli Tikka　71
Paneer Tikka　73
Peas, Broccoli & Mushroom
Au Gratin　74
Tinda Tandoori　75
Vegetables on a bed of Spinach　76

NON-VEGETARIAN

Chicken Grilled with
Orange Juice　58
Tandoori Chicken　61
Oven Fried Fish　64
Herbed Baked Fish　64
Fish Tikka　65
Baked Chicken with Spinach　67
Tandoori Fish　70
Grilled Sesame Chicken　72

SNACKS & STARTERS　77

VEGETARIAN

Mushroom Balls　78
Instant Dhokla　81
Stuffed Khandvi　82
Spiced Baby Corns　84
Fruity Cherry Tomatoes　84
Momos　86
Instant Suji Utthapams　88
Spiced Button Idlis　90
Grilled Curd Cheese Fingers　92
Sesame Potato Fingers　92

NON-VEGETARIAN

Low Cal Chicken Club
Sandwiches　80
Chicken Fingers　83
Methi Chicken Chat　83
Chicken Canapes　85
Mince Dumplings　87
Paper Fried Chicken　91
Chicken Momos　86
Honeyed Barbecued Chicken
Fish or Prawns　95

Mango Submarine Special   93
Vegetable Gold Coins   94
Oil free Baby Corn Canapes   96
Unfried Chilly Potatoes   97

Barbecued Chicken Drumsticks   95
Grilled Chilli Prawns   100
Mutton Balls   98

SOUPS & SALADS   101

VEGETARIAN

Tomato & Coriander Shorba   102
Kali Mirch Jeera Rasam   103
Broccoli & Bean Salad
in Mustard Dressing   104
Green Papaya Salad   105
Potato Salad   107
Fruity Salad in Orange Dressing   107
Cottage Cheese Boats   111
Sprouts in Spicy Honey
Dressing   111

NON-VEGETARIAN

Creamy Chicken Salad   105
Chicken Hot & Sour Soup   106
Clear Chicken &
Mushroom Soup   108
Chicken Flower Soup   108
Warm Stir Fried Salad   110

LOW CALORIE DESSERTS   112

WITH EGGS

Chocolate Chip Pudding   113
Apple Meringue Pudding   114
Steamed Caramel Custard   115
Queen Pudding   116
Glazed Pineapple Pudding   118
Orange Cake with
Orange Sauce   124
Apple & Date Pudding   126

WITHOUT EGGS

Chocolate Souffle   120
Mango cheese cake   117
Apple Crumble   121
Light Chocolate Sandesh   121
Crunchy Bread Pudding   122
Fresh Peaches in Sauce   123
Juicy Fruit Jelly   125

Calorie Guidance

VEGETABLES	Calories
Brinjal, raw 100 g	24
Beetroot, cooked ½ cup	34
Cabbage, shredded, raw ½ cup	12
Carrot, raw 1 large	42
Cauliflower, cooked ½ cup	15
Coriander leaves (dhania), raw 100 g	48
Corn (maize), tender, boiled 1	84
Cucumber ½ medium	6
Drumstick, raw 100 g	26
Lady's fingers (okra; bhindi) 8 or 9 pods	28
Lettuce 3 small leaves	5
Onion, mature, raw 1 average	45
Peas, green, cooked ½ cup	56
Potato, boiled 1 medium	83
Pumpkin, cooked ½ cup	33
Spinach, cooked ½ cup	23
Tomato, raw 1 medium	20

FRUITS	Calories
Apple 1 medium	66
Banana 1	132
Figs, Fresh 3 small	79
Grapefruit ½ medium	72
Grapes 22-24	70
Guava 1 medium	51
Lemon, sour 100 g	42
Sweet Lime (mausambi) 1 average	63
Mango, Alphonso 1	122

FRUITS	Calories
Melon ½ medium	37
Orange 1 medium	68
Papaya 1/3 medium	50
Peach, fresh 1 medium	32
Pear 1	84
Pineapple 1 slice	44
Plum 1	30
Pomegranate 100 g	90
Watermelon cubes 100 g	28

CEREAL & CEREAL FOODS	Calories
Bajra flour 30 g 1 small chappati	108
Barley, pearled dry 2 tbsp	99
Jowar flour 30 g 1 small chappati	106
Macaroni, cooked 2/3 cup	107
Maize flour 30 g 1 chappati	102
Oat Meal, porridge cooked 1 cup	148
Rice, milled, boiled 1 cup	138
Wheat bread 1 slice	75
Wheat chappati (30 g flour) 1 thin	70
Wheat parantha 60 g (with 2 tsp fat) 1	256
Wheat khakhra (15 g flour) 1	50

MILK & MILK PRODUCTS	Calories
Buttermilk 1 cup	62
Cheese, Cheddar 28 g	111
Cheese, cottage 1 rounded tbsp	27
Cream, light 2 tbsp	56

MILK & MILK PRODUCTS	Calories
Curds, buffalo milk 1 cup	182
Ice Cream 100 g	96
Milk, buffalo's 1 cup	206
Milk, buffalo's skimmed 1 cup	78
Milk, cow's 1 cup	160
Milk, cow's skimmed 1 cup	70
Milk, condensed, sweetened 1 tbsp	62

FATS & OILS	Calories
Butter 1 tsp	36
Ghee (clarified butter) 1 tsp	45
Oil, groundnut 1 tbsp	135
Oil, til 1 tbsp	126

PULSES	Calories
Bengal gram roasted 100 g	369
Bengal gram (channa dal)	
Black gram (urad dal)	200 g
Green gram (moong dal)	1 cup 105
Lentil (masoor dal)	cooked
Red gram (tur dal)	thin dal

BEVERAGES	Calories
Cocoa, 1 tbsp	
with cow's milk 1 cup	224
Coffee, 1 cup	
with cow's milk 2 tbsp	
and sugar 2 tsp	60
Tea, 1 cup	
with cow's milk 2 tbsp	
and sugar 2 tsp	60

DRIED FRUITS & NUTS	Calories
Currants ½ cup	268
Figs, dried 2 small	81
Raisins, seedless 1 tbsp	27
Almonds 12-15	90
Cashew nuts 6-8	88
Coconut, fresh 1 piece	54
Coconut water 1 glass	46
Peanuts (groundnuts)	
roasted 1 tbsp	86
Pistachio nuts 30	88
Walnuts 8 halves	128

SUGAR, CHOCOLATE etc.	Calories
Chocolate, nut 1 piece	142
Glucose 1 tbsp	45
Honey 1 tbsp	60
Jaggery 1 tbsp	56
Sugar, white	
granular 1 tsp level	20
Sugar, cube 1 piece	24
Aspartame 36 mg	0.14

DESSERTS	Calories
Cake, sponge 50 g	153
Custard, baked 157	205
Jelly 65 g	65
Pie (fruit) 160 g	377

Low Calorie Indian Recipes

CURRIES & WET DISHES

Paneer Dakshin Style

Serves 5-6 *cal/serving* 116

Paneer in a tangy sauce flavoured with mustard seeds & curry leaves.

200 gm paneer - cut into ¼" thick slices and then diagonally into triangles
juice of 1 lemon (2 tbsp)
½ cup coconut milk
½ tsp sugar, optional

PRESSURE COOK TOGETHER
4 large tomatoes - chopped roughly
2 green chillies - chopped roughly
1½" piece ginger - chopped, 8-10 flakes garlic - chopped
1 tsp salt, or to taste
1 cup water

BAGHAR/TADKA
1 tsp oil
1 tsp sarson (black mustard seeds)
2 whole, dry red chillies
10-15 curry leaves

1. In a pressure cooker, cook together tomatoes, green chillies, ginger, garlic and salt with 1 cup water on high flame to give 2 whistles.
2. After the pressure drops, cool and make a paste in a blender.
3. Strain the tomato paste back in the pressure cooker, boil it and add the lemon juice, then add the coconut milk to it. Boil it. Simmer for 4-5 minutes till gravy turns a little thick. Add sugar if the gravy tastes too sour.
4. Grate 2 pieces of paneer and add to the gravy. Add the rest of the paneer pieces and curry leaves to the gravy. Remove from fire.
5. Heat a small heavy bottomed kadhai with oil. Reduce heat. Add mustard seeds. Wait for 30 seconds to make them crackle. Add whole red chillies. Stir. Remove from fire. Add a few curry leaves.
6. Add the baghar to the paneer gravy and mix. Serve hot.

Note: To take out coconut milk, grate ¼ of a fresh coconut and add 1 cup hot water to it. Blend in a mixer and squeeze through a muslin to get coconut milk. You may use desiccated coconut powder instead of fresh coconut. Simply fill ½ cup with desiccated coconut (nariyal ka powder) and fill the cup with water. Mix well and use instead of fresh coconut milk.

Gatte ki Subzi

cal/serving 129   Serves 4-5

GATTE
1 cup besan (gram flour)
a pinch of soda bicarb (mitha soda), 1 tsp salt, ½ tsp ajwain (carom seeds)
½ tsp haldi, ½ tsp red chilli powder, ½ tsp jeera powder (cumin powder)
½ tsp saunf (fennel) - coarsely powdered
½ tsp dhania powder, ½ tsp garam masala powder
½ tsp ginger paste, ½ tsp green chilli paste (optional)
1 tbsp oil
2-3 tbsp curd, approx.

GRAVY (MIX TOGETHER)
1 cup curd (preferably 1-2 days old)
2 tsp besan
½ tsp haldi powder, 1½ tsp salt
¼ tsp ginger paste, ½ tsp green chilli paste (optional)
1 tbsp oil, ½ tsp jeera, 8-10 curry leaves
3-4 laung (cloves), 2 moti illaichi (cardamoms)
½ tsp red chilli powder
1 large or 2 medium tomatoes - pureed and strained
some fresh chopped coriander - for garnishing

1. To make gatte, mix together all ingredients except curd. Add enough curd to get a soft dough like a chappati dough. Do not add any water.
2. With oiled hands, roll out thin fingers 3"-4" long, like cylinders.
3. Boil 5 cups of water. Keep the gatte in a stainless steel round strainer and keep the strainer on the pan of boiling water and cover with a lid.
4. Steam gatte for 5-7 minutes. Let them cool. Later cut them into rounds of ½" thickness. Keep aside.
5. To prepare the curry, mix together curd, besan, haldi, salt, ginger paste & green chilli paste. Add 1 cup water. Beat well & sieve to remove any lumps.
6. Heat oil. Add jeera, when jeera turns golden, add curry leaves. Add laung and moti illaichi. Stir fry for 1 minute.
7. Reduce heat. Add red chilli powder.
8. Add curd mixture. Go on stirring till it boils.
9. Add pureed tomatoes (should be very smooth, so strain to make it smooth).
10. Give 2-3 boils, (can add more water if more gravy is needed). Add gatte.
11. Cover, lower heat. Simmer for 4-5 minutes. Serve hot garnished with hara dhania.

Rajasthani Bharwan Mirch

Serves 5-6   *cal/serving*   119

The chillies used here are the thick large green chillies, which are not very hot.

150 gms (10) green chillies (large, not very hot ones)

STUFFING
½ tsp rai (mustard seeds), ½ tsp methi dana (fenugreek seeds)
a pinch of hing (asafoetida)
4 tbsp besan (gram flour)
½ tsp haldi, 2 tsp amchoor powder
1 tsp salt, 1 tsp dhania powder, 1 tsp garam masala powder
1 tbsp oil

GRAVY
2 tbsp til (white), 4 tbsp grated fresh coconut
2 tbsp oil
½ tsp jeera (cumin seeds), ½ tsp rai (mustard seeds)
¼ tsp hing
6 laung (cloves), 4-5 curry leaves
1 tsp salt, ½ tsp garam masala
½ tsp each - red chilli powder, haldi, dhania powder
1 cup imli (tamarind) water, 1 cup water
½ tsp sugar (optional)

1. Slit chillies on one side. If they are very long, they can be cut into 2 pieces vertically.
2. To prepare the stuffing, heat oil. Add methi dana & rai. When it splutters, add hing.
3. Add besan & all other ingredients under stuffing & cook, stirring continuously on low heat till a nice aroma comes. Cool & stuff in the chillies and keep aside.
4. For the gravy, dry roast til & coconut lightly. Grind to a paste (use little water if needed) and keep aside.
5. Heat 2 tbsp oil. Add jeera and rai. When they splutter, add hing. Fry for 1 minute. Add laung and curry leaves.
6. Add stuffed chillies and fry till nearly roasted.
7. Add ground paste of til and coconut. Fry for 1-2 minutes.
8. Add salt and all masalas along with imli water and 1 cup water.
9. Cook covered till chillies turn tender & a thick gravy remains. Add sugar if the gravy is too sour.
10. Garnish with fresh dhania and serve hot with boiled rice.

Dal Makhani

cal/serving 74   *Serves 8*

Delicious dal without makhan (butter)!

1½ cups kaali dal (saboot urad)
1 large onion - grated, 8-10 flakes garlic - crushed
2 tsp salt, or to taste, 3/4 tsp red chilli powder
6 tbsp tomato puree, 1 tsp jeera powder, 2 tsp tandoori masala
1" piece ginger - cut Into thin long pieces, ½ cup milk

1. Soak the kaali dal for 3-4 hours in warm water or overnight.
2. Pressure cook dal with grated onion, garlic, salt, red chilli powder and enough water (about 5 cups) to give 1 whistle and keep on low flame for 40 minutes.
3. Remove from fire. After the pressure drops, mash it with a ladle (karchhi).
4. Add tomato puree, jeera powder and tandoori masala. Pressure cook for 2 or 3 whistles. Remove from fire. Let the pressure drop by itself.
5. Add ½ cup milk to get the right consistency. Cook for 3-4 minutes on low heat. Serve garnished with ginger juliennes.

Oil free Matar Paneer

cal/serving 87   *Serves 4*

100 gms paneer - cut into 1" pieces
1 cup peas, 6 tbsp tomato puree, 1 tsp salt, ½ tsp haldi
1 tsp jeera powder, 1 tsp dhania powder, ½ tsp red chilli powder (degi mirch)
1 tbsp chopped coriander, to garnish, 1/3 tsp garam masala

GRIND TO A PASTE
1 large onion, 1" piece ginger, 5-6 garlic flakes

1. Cut onions, garlic and ginger. Grind to a paste in the mixer with 2-3 tsp water.
2. In a pressure cooker, add the onion-garlic paste, cook on low flame for about 3-4 minutes till water evaporates and it turns dry.
3. Add tomato puree.
4. Add salt, haldi, jeera powder, dhania and red chilli powder, stir for 2 minutes.
5. Add peas. Stir for 1-2 minutes.
6. Add enough water to get the gravy consistency, (1½-2 cups) and pressure cook for 2 whistles. Remove from fire. Let the pressure drop by itself. Add paneer pieces and garam masala. Give 2-3 quick boils. Serve garnished with coriander.

Fish Creole

Picture on facing page   *Serves 3-4*   *cal/serving 91*

Delicious tomato fish. Prawns can be made in the same way.

300 gms fish - cut into 2" pieces, preferably fillet and boneless, however other fish can also be used
1 tbsp besan & juice of ½ lemon, to wash fish
1 tbsp oil
1 medium onion - chopped finely
1 large capsicum - chopped finely
3/4 cup tomato puree
1 tsp kasoori methi (dry fenugreek leaves)
5 tbsp chilli sauce
1 tbsp vinegar
1 tsp salt, or to taste, 1 tsp sugar
2 tsp cornflour dissolved in ¼ cup water

TO SERVE
3/4 cup chopped coriander
3-4 cups boiled rice

1. Rub the fish with 1 tbsp besan and some lemon juice to remove the fishy odour. Wash and pat dry on a kitchen towel or with a tissue napkin.
2. In a nonstick pan heat oil. Add onion and capsicum. Saute for 2 minutes on low heat.
3. Add tomato puree, kasoori methi, chilli sauce, vinegar, salt and sugar. Stir for 1-2 minutes.
4. Add ½ cup water. Give one boil.
5. Add fish in a single layer.
6. Cook uncovered for 6-7 minutes. (Turn over fish after 3-4 minutes) or till fish is thoroughly cooked.
7. Remove fish pieces with a slotted spoon on to a serving dish.
8. To the gravy in the nonstick pan, add cornflour dissolved in ¼ cup of water.
9. Give one boil. Cook for a minute on low heat. Pour over fish.
10. Serve with boiled rice to which a lot of coriander is added at the time of serving and mixed well.

Fish Creole ➤

Dapka Kadhi

Picture on page 89   *Serves 5*   *cal/serving* 105

Gujarati kadhi with unfried moong dumplings. Enjoy without guilt with boiled rice!

KADHI
2 tbsp besan (gram flour)
2 cups fresh curd
2 green chillies & 1" piece ginger - chopped, ground or crushed to a paste together
2 tbsp chopped coriander
½ tsp sugar, 2 tsp salt, or to taste

DAPKAS (DUMPLINGS)
½ cup dhuli moong dal (split green gram) - soaked for 4-5 hours
¼ tsp eno fruit salt
1 tsp oil
1 green chilli - finely chopped, ½" piece ginger - finely chopped
¼ tsp sugar, ½ tsp salt, or to taste

TEMPERING
1 tbsp oil
3/4 tsp jeera (cumin seeds), 3/4 tsp rai (mustard seeds)
a pinch hing (asafoetida), 1 dry, red chilli - broken into pieces

1. For the dapkas, soak the moong dal in lukewarm water for 4-5 hours or overnight. Drain well to remove all water. Grind the soaked moong dal to a very fine paste in a small spice grinder.
2. Add the oil, green chillies, ginger, sugar, eno fruit salt and salt. Beat well for 2-3 minutes till light. Keep the dapka batter aside.
3. For the kadhi, mix the besan, curds and 3 cups of water till smooth.
4. Add the green chilli-ginger paste, fresh coriander, sugar and salt and put to boil in a kadhai. Simmer for a while stirring occasionally.
5. When the kadhi is boiling, test the batter of the dapkas by adding a little dapka batter using your fingers to form 1 dumpling (pakodi). Keep the kadhi boiling. If the dapka floats after while, put more pakodis. If it does not, beat the batter some more to make it lighter. Add spoonfuls of batter to get more dapkas. Cook on low heat for 8-10 minutes till the dapkas float and also get cooked. Remove kadhi from fire and keep aside.
6. Heat oil for tempering. Reduce heat. Add jeera, rai and hing. When jeera turns golden, remove from fire and mix in the red chilli bits.
7. Add the tempering to the hot kadhi. Sprinkle fresh coriander. Serve.

Kashmiri Chicken Yakhni

cal/serving 155   *Serves 8*

Delicious chicken cooked in white curd gravy. For mutton yakhni, pressure cook the mutton yakhni after adding the curd, to give 4-5 whistles.

1 chicken - cut into 8 pieces
2 tbsp oil
2 tej patta (bay leaves), 5 laung (cloves)
3½ tsp saunf (fennel) powder
2 tsp sonth powder (dry ginger powder)
1¼ tsp salt, or to taste
2½ cups curd - well beaten
1 tsp garam masala (optional)
1 moti illaichi and 4 chhoti illaichi (green cardamoms) - coarsely powdered

1. Heat oil in a non stick pan or kadhai. Add tej patta and laung. Fry for 2-3 minutes.
2. Add chicken. Fry for 3-4 minutes.
3. Add saunf, sonth and salt. Fry for 2-3 minutes.
4. Add crushed cardamoms.
5. Reduce heat. Add beaten curd. Mix well. Keep stirring till it boils.
6. Cover and simmer on low heat till chicken is well cooked and some gravy remains. Sprinkle garam masala and serve.

Khatti Machli

Serves 4   *cal/serving*   158

300 gms fish, 1 tbsp oil
3/4 tsp jeera (cumin seeds), 3-4 laung (cloves)
1 moti illaichi (cardamom), 1" dalchini (cinnamon), 1 tej patta (bay leaf)
¼ tsp hing (asafoetida)
1 tsp ginger paste, 3-4 green chillies - chopped
3/4 tsp salt, 1 tsp red chilli powder (degi mirch)
1½ tsp saunf (fennel powder), ½ tsp sonth (dry ginger powder), ½ tsp haldi
1½ cups thick curd - well beaten

1. Heat oil. Add jeera & all the whole garam masalas - laung, moti illaichi, dalchini and tej patta. When jeera turns light golden add hing. Stir fry for a few seconds.
2. Add ginger paste and green chillies. Fry for ½ minute.
3. Reduce heat. Add all seasonings and curd. Keep stirring till it boils.
4. Add fish. Cover with a tight lid. Simmer for 8-10 minutes. Remove from fire. Sprinkle some garam masala and amchoor. Serve hot.

Chicken in Tomato Gravy

Serves 8   *cal/serving*   148

1 chicken (approx. 800 gm) - cut into pieces of your choice
3 large tomatoes - grind to a puree
1 small onion - grated or ground to a paste
1 tsp dhania powder, 1 tsp garam masala powder
1 tsp sugar (optional), 1 tsp jeera (cumin seeds) powder, 1½ tsp salt, or to taste
2 tsp oil
1 tsp kasoori methi (dry fenugreek leaves)
a pinch of orange red colour

1. Heat 2 tsp oil in a non stick kadhai or pan. Add onion and fry till light brown.
2. Add chicken. Bhuno for 3-4 minutes.
3. Add tomato puree and all ingredients except kasoori methi and colour. Mix well.
4. Cover and simmer for 15-20 minutes or till chicken is well cooked.
5. Add kasoori methi and colour. Give 1-2 boils. Mix well.
6. Serve hot garnished with fresh coriander leaves.

Chicken Malgoba Curry

cal/serving   172   Serves 8

A very simple but delicious curry.

1 chicken (approx. 800 gm) - cut into 8 pieces
1 tbsp oil
2 large onions - ground to a paste, 2 tsp ginger paste
1½ tsp salt, 1 tsp haldi, 1 tsp dhania powder, 1 tsp red chilli powder
2 cups curd mixed with 2 tsp maida (plain flour)
1 tsp garam masala

1. In a nonstick pan heat oil. Add onions and stir till light brown.
2. Add ginger paste, salt, haldi, dhania powder and red chilli powder.
3. Add chicken. Stir fry for 3-4 minutes.
4. Beat curd well. Add maida and mix well with the curd.
5. Add curd to chicken and keep stirring till it boils. Cover and simmer for 8-10 minutes or till chicken is cooked. Add garam masala. Mix.
6. Serve hot, garnished with fresh ginger strips and coriander.

Red Dhania Chicken

cal/serving   150   Serves 8

A quick, simple and delicious curry with the predominant flavour of coriander.
Cooked without oil.

1 chicken (800 gm) - cut into pieces of your choice
1 cup tomato puree
1-2 tsp tomato ketchup
½ cup dhania powder
2 tsp garlic paste, 2 tsp ginger paste
1½ tsp salt, 1 tsp garam masala, 1½ tsp red chilli powder

GARNISHING
lots of fresh chopped dhania

1. Heat a non stick pan. Add tomato puree and all the other ingredients below it. Mix.
2. Add chicken. Stir for 3-4 minutes.
3. Add ½ cup water. Cover. Lower heat and let it cook for 4-5 minutes.
4. Stir well and let it simmer covered till chicken is tender.
5. Increase heat and dry as much as you like (you can keep a little gravy or make it dry). Serve hot sprinkled with lots of fresh chopped dhania.

Anaarkali Aloo

Picture on page 79   *Serves 8*   *cal/serving* 73

Juice of red kandhari anaar (fresh pomegranate) is added to give the curry
an intriguing flavour.

250 gm baby potatoes or regular potatoes
¼ cup tomato puree
1½ tbsp khus khus - soaked in 2 tbsp hot milk
1 tbsp oil
2 onions - ground to a paste
3/4 tsp salt, or to taste
½ tsp deghi mirch or Kashmiri laal mirch powder
1 tsp kasoori methi (dried fenugreek leaves)
1 cup anaar ke daane from kandhari anaar (red pomegranate)
¼ cup curd, ½ tsp cornflour or maida

GARNISH
1" piece ginger - cut into juliennes or match sticks
1 tbsp chopped coriander leaves

1. Boil potatoes. Peel and keep aside. If using regular potatoes, boil small ones and cut them into 4 pieces.
2. Grind khus khus along with milk to a smooth paste.
3. Keeping aside 3-4 tbsp anaar ke daane (pomegranate kernels) for garnishing, take out juice of anaar by grinding the kernels (anaar ke daane) in a mixer-blender without any water. Strain to get ½ cup juice.
4. Heat oil in a kadhai. Add onion paste and cook for 2-3 minutes till water dries completely.
5. In a bowl, mix together - tomato puree, khuskhus paste, and 1 cup water. Add this to the dried onion paste in the kadhai. Bring to a boil.
6. Add boiled potatoes, salt & chilli powder.
7. Add juice of pomegranate.
8. Add kasoori methi.
9. Reduce heat. Mix cornflour to curd and beat well to make it smooth. Add to the potato gravy.
10. Let the gravy boil on low heat, stirring continuously. Cover and simmer for 7-8 minutes.
11. Serve hot garnished with anaar ke daane, ginger juliennes and coriander.

Handi Channas without Oil

cal/serving 117   *Serves 4-5*

2 cups kabuli channa (chick peas)
2 moti illaichi (brown cardamoms), 3-4 laung (cloves)
1 large onion - finely chopped
1 tsp garlic paste, 1 tsp ginger paste
1½ - 2 tsp salt, or to taste
4 tsp dhania powder
3 tsp channa masala powder
2 tsp bhuna jeera powder
½ tsp garam masala
½ tsp red chilli powder
3 tsp imli (tamarind) pulp or squeeze out pulp from a marble size ball of tamarind

GARNISHING
1 tomato - cut into 8 pieces
1-2 green chillies - cut lengthwise into half
a few ginger juliennes (match sticks)

1. Soak the channas overnight.
2. Next morning drain water. Put in a pressure cooker. Add 4 cups fresh water. Add finely chopped onion, moti illaichi, laung, garlic paste and ginger paste. Pressure cook to give 1 whistle and keep on low flame or 15-20 minutes.
3. After the pressure drops open the cooker. Add salt, dhania powder, channa masala, jeera powder, garam masala, red chilli and the tamarind pulp to the cooked channas. Mash the channas a bit.
4. Again pressure cook to give 2-3 whistles.
5. Serve hot garnished with ginger match sticks, tomatoes & green chillies.

Quick Unfried Dahivada

Serves 4-6　　　　　　　　　*cal/serving　60*

Prepare at least an hour before serving, for the bread to soak the dahi.

2 slices of fresh bread, preferably whole wheat bread

RAITA
1½ cups thick curd (of toned milk) - beat till smooth
½ tsp bhuna jeera powder
½ tsp red chilli powder
1 tbsp finely chopped fresh coriander
¼ tsp kala namak
3/4 tsp salt, or to taste

KHATTI MEETHI CHUTNEY
1 tbsp amchoor (dry mango powder)
3 tbsp sugar
¼ tsp red chilli powder
¼ tsp garam masala
¼ tsp bhuna jeera (roasted cumin) powder
salt to taste

1. Whip curd. Mix all spices and fresh coriander to make a raita.
2. Cut sides of bread and arrange in a shallow dish.
3. Pour the dahi on it to cover completely. Let the dahi cover the empty spaces of the dish also.
4. Sprinkle red chilli powder and bhuna jeera powder on the dahi.
5. With a spoon, pour the chutney on it, in circles.
6. Garnish with bhuna jeera, red chilli powder and fresh coriander.
7. Leave in the fridge for atleast ½ hour for the bread to soak the curd.
8. Serve with extra chutney.

Note: Although these are not individual pieces of dahi badas, it tastes very much like dahi badas. I am positive you will like it!

Low Calorie Indian Recipes

DRY & SEMI DRY DISHES

Avial

Picture on facing page   *Serves 4*   *cal/serving   105*

A South Indian preparation of mixed vegetables in coconut masala. Desiccated coconut has been used so there is hardly any fat in it.

1 large capsicum - cut into 1" pieces
3 carrots - cut into 4 pieces lengthwise and then into 1" long fingers
100 gm (10-12) french beans - cut into 1" pieces
½ cup desiccated coconut
1½ cups (300 ml) water
2 tbsp oil
½ tsp sarson (mustard seeds)
1½" piece ginger - peeled and chopped
3 flakes garlic - chopped
1 large onion - chopped
2 tsp dhania powder (ground coriander)
½ tsp garam masala
½ tsp haldi (turmeric powder)
1 tsp salt, or to taste
1 green chilli - cut lengthwise into thin pieces

1. Blend the desiccated coconut and water together in a mixer till smooth. Keep the coconut milk aside.
2. Heat oil in a pressure cooker. Add mustard seeds. Let them splutter.
3. Add the chopped ginger-garlic and fry for about 1 minute.
4. Add the onion and stir fry until golden brown.
5. Add dhania powder, garam masala, haldi and salt. Stir for a few seconds.
6. Add vegetables to the cooker and stir for 2-3 minutes.
7. Add the prepared coconut milk and green chilli. Pressure cook to give 1 whistle on high flame. Remove from fire.

Avial ➤

Kadhai Chicken

Picture on cover   *Serves 6*   *cal/serving*   191

Crushed coriander seeds add the crunch to this chicken dish, whereas shredded ginger and dry fenugreek seeds impart their flavour to the chicken.

1 medium sized (800 gm) chicken - cut into 8 pieces
1 whole pod or 15-20 flakes garlic - crushed & chopped
6 whole, dry, red chillies
2 tbsp saboot dhania (coriander seeds)
3" piece ginger - finely shredded
½ cup green coriander - chopped
½ kg (6-7 large) tomatoes - chopped
2 green chillies - sliced lengthways
1 tbsp kasoori methi (dried fenugreek leaves)
salt to taste
2 tbsp oil
½ tsp garam masala

1. Clean and cut chicken into 8 pieces. Wash well and pat dry on a clean kitchen towel.
2. Heat red chillies on a tawa till slightly crisp and dry.
3. Pound or crush whole red chillies and saboot dhania to a coarse powder.
4. Heat oil in a nonstick kadhai. Reduce flame. Add crushed garlic and saute over medium heat until it starts to change colour.
5. Add pounded dhania & red chillies, stir for 30 seconds. Add chopped tomatoes and bring to a boil.
6. Add ½ of the ginger and ½ of the coriander leaves. Reduce the heat and let the tomatoes simmer until soft. Add salt.
7. Add the chicken, cook on low flame with the lid covered, stirring occasionally, till the chicken is tender, or add ½ cup water and pressure cook to give 1 whistle and keep on low heat for 1 minute.
8. Add kasoori methi and garam masala.
9. Uncover and stir fry until the masala coats the chicken. Remove from fire.
10. Garnish with the remaining ginger, sliced chillies & coriander leaves.

Dahi Masala Mushrooms

cal/serving 73   Serves 4

Mushrooms have a low fat content. They are a rich source of vitamins and minerals.

200 gms (1 pack fresh mushrooms) - each cut into 4-5 'T' shaped slices
2 tsp oil, 1 tsp ajwain (carom seeds)
2 onions - chopped finely, 1" piece ginger, 2 green chillies - chopped finely
½ tsp garam masala, ½ tsp red chilli powder, 1 tsp dhania (coriander) powder
3/4 cup fresh curd of skimmed milk
1 tsp salt, or to taste
greens of 1 spring onion or ¼ cup chopped coriander

1. Heat oil in a non-stick pan. Add ajwain. Cook for 30 seconds.
2. Add onions, green chillies and ginger. Cook till onions turn light brown in colour.
3. Add mushrooms. Mix well. Cook covered, for about 5 minutes till they leave water. Uncover and stir for 2-3 minutes.
4. Reduce heat. Add chilli powder and coriander powder.
5. Blend in beaten curd, garam masala & salt.
6. Cook till curd dries up a little & coats the mushrooms. Add spring onion greens or fresh coriander. Add deseeded fresh red chillies if you like. Serve hot.

Baked Baingan ka Bharta

cal/serving 32   Serves 4

1 large round baingan - roasted on a gas flame
1 onion - finely chopped, ½" piece ginger - chopped finely
2 tomatoes - finely chopped
2 green chillies - finely chopped
½ tsp red chilli powder, ½ tsp garam masala, ¼ tsp amchoor
1½ tsp salt, or to taste, ½ tsp bhuna jeera
1 tsp oil
2 tbsp chopped hara dhania for garnishing

1. Rub a little oil over the baingan and roast over a gas flame until the skin gets charred and starts to peel off and the flesh is soft.
2. Remove the charred skin of baingan. Wash and mash the flesh with a fork. Mix all ingredients, including 1 tsp oil, with the baingans in a large, but shallow oven proof dish.
3. Preheat oven at 200°C. Bake bharta for 40 minutes, stirring in between. Serve.

Palak-Methi Chicken

Serves 8　　　　　　　*cal/serving*　188

The addition of fresh methi to spinach makes the dish tastier.

**1 chicken (700-800 gm) - cut into 8 pieces
500 gm palak (spinach), 250 gm fresh methi (fenugreek greens)
2-3 onions - chopped finely
3 tbsp ginger-garlic-green chilli paste
1 large tomato - chopped
½ cup thick curd - beaten well till smooth
1 tsp garam masala
1 tsp chilli powder
salt to taste
½ cup milk or water
2 tbsp oil**

1. Sprinkle little salt on methi leaves. Keep aside for 15 minutes. Squeeze to remove bitterness from the leaves. Wash leaves and keep aside.
2. Cut the stems of spinach and chop the leaves finely. Wash leaves in plenty of water, changing water several times.
3. Heat oil in a heavy bottomed pan. Add onions. Stir fry till light brown.
4. Add the ginger-garlic-chilli paste. Cook for 1 minute.
5. Add tomato. Cook for 1 minute, till it turns mushy.
6. Add curd, salt, chilli powder, garam masala and cook on high flame for 4-5 minutes.
7. Squeeze out all the excess water from spinach & methi leaves. Add to the masala. Cook on high flame till all the excess water evaporates.
8. Now add the washed chicken pieces and bhuno or stir fry on high flame stirring constantly.
9. Cook till water evaporates and the masala sticks to the chicken pieces. Add milk or water. Reduce heat. Cover and cook till the chicken is tender.
10. Remove cover and again cook for 2 to 3 minutes or till chicken pieces are coated with spinach masala. Serve hot.

Palak Makai ki Subzi

Picture on back cover   Serves 4   *cal/serving*   129

500 gms paalak (spinach)
1 cup cooked corn kernels
1" piece ginger - grated
1- 2 tbsp oil
2 moti elaichi (black cardamoms)
1" stick dalchini (cinnamon)
5-6 flakes garlic - crushed to a rough paste
2 onions - finely sliced
3 tomatoes - chopped
3/4 tsp haldi (turmeric powder)
1 tsp dhania powder (ground coriander)
½ tsp red chilli powder
½ tsp garam masala
1 tsp salt, or to taste

1. Boil whole corn or frozen corn kernels with ¼ tsp haldi, 2 tsp sugar and 1 tsp salt to get soft, yellow, sweetish corn.
2. Heat oil. Reduce heat. Add moti illaichi and dalchini. Wait for a minute.
3. Add garlic and cook till it starts to change colour.
4. Add onions and stir fry till golden. Reduce heat.
5. Add haldi powder, dhania powder, chilli powder, garam masala and salt. Mix well on low heat for a minute.
6. Add ginger. Stir for a few seconds.
7. Add corn. Stir fry for 2-3 minutes.
8. Add spinach. Continue cooking, without covering, for about 10 minutes, till the spinach gets wilted and is well blended with the corn.
9. Add tomatoes and stir fry for 3-4 minutes. Garnish with ginger match sticks and serve hot with chapattis.

Vegetable Jalfrazie

Serves 5-6   *cal/serving* 50

4 tomatoes - roasted, peeled and chopped
1 tbsp oil, 1 large onion - chopped, 3-4 flakes garlic - chopped
2 carrots - cut into 1½" long, thin fingers
4-6 baby corns - slit into 2 pieces lengthwise, 1 capsicum - cut into thin fingers
1½ tsp salt, or to taste, 1" piece ginger - chopped
1 cup peas - boiled, 1 tbsp tomato puree, 1 tbsp vinegar
3/4 tsp black pepper powder, 1 tsp sugar, 1 tsp oregano (optional)
2 tsp cornflour dissolved in ½ cup water

1. Pierce a tomato on a fork deeply and hold it over a naked flame for 2-3 minutes to blacken and loosen the skin. Peel and chop the roasted tomatoes.
2. Heat oil in a kadhai. Add garlic and onion. Stir fry till soft. Add carrots and baby corns. Stir fry for 2 minutes on low heat. Add ½ cup water and salt.
3. Cook for 5 minutes on low heat till the vegetables get cooked. Add capsicum and stir for 1 minute.
4. Add the chopped tomatoes and ginger. Stir for 3-4 minutes. Add oregano.
5. Add tomato puree, vinegar, black pepper powder and 1 tsp of sugar. Mix well.
6. Add the boiled peas. Mix well. Add cornflour paste and cook till sauce turns thick. Serve hot.

Matar Dhania Wale

Serves 4-5   *cal/serving* 87

2 cups shelled peas
1 tbsp oil
a pinch of hing, ½ tsp jeera, ¼ tsp kalonji, ½ tsp salt, or to taste
1 firm tomato - cut into 8 pieces and pulp removed

DHANIA CHUTNEY
2 cups coriander leaves, 4 flakes garlic, 1½" piece of ginger, 2 green chillies
juice of 1 lemon, 1 tomato, ½ tsp salt, or to taste

1. Grind together all the ingredients of the dhania chutney.
2. Heat 1 tbsp oil in the pressure cooker. Add hing, jeera and kalonji.
3. When jeera turns brown, add peas. Fry for 2-3 minutes.
4. Add dhania chutney to the peas and mix well. Add salt. Pressure cook to give 1 whistle. Open the cooker after the pressure drops. Mix in the tomato. Serve hot.

Kashmiri Danival Chicken Korma

cal/serving   157   Serves 8

Chicken with coriander.

1 chicken (800 gms) - cut into pieces of your choice
2 tbsp oil, 2 onions - ground to a paste
1½ cups curd - well beaten till smooth
1¾ tsp salt, 2 tsp dhania powder
1 tsp saunf (fennel powder)
1 tsp sonth (dry ginger powder)
8 chhoti illaichi (green cardamoms) - powdered
½ tsp garam masala, ½ cup fresh coriander leaves - chopped finely

1. Heat oil in a non stick pan or kadhai. Add onion paste and stir fry on low heat till brown.
2. Add chicken and fry for 2-3 minutes. Lower heat.
3. Add curd, saunf, sonth, salt and dhania powder. Stir continuously on low heat till it boils. Cook covered till chicken gets cooked and a little gravy remains.
4. Add garam masala, powdered illaichi and fresh dhania. Cook for 1-2 minutes. Serve hot.

Elaichi Murg

cal/serving   175   Serves 4

A very popular Sindhi recipe.

500 gms chicken - cut into small pieces
1 tbsp oil, 1 onion - chopped fine, ¾ tsp salt
½ tsp pepper, ¾ tsp chhoti elaichi (green cardamom) powder
1 tomato - finely chopped, ½ tsp garam masala

1. Heat oil in a nonstick pan. Add onion and fry till light brown.
2. Add chicken, salt, pepper, garam masala and ½ tsp elaichi powder. Fry for 2-3 minutes.
3. Add finely chopped tomato. Fry for 1-2 minutes.
4. Cover. Lower heat and cook till chicken is tender.
5. Increase heat and make it nearly dry.
6. Sprinkle ¼ tsp elaichi powder on top. Garnish with chopped dhania and serve.

Kesari Dahi Waale Aloo

Serves 4   *cal/serving*   *138*

250 gm, about 15 baby potatoes or 4 regular potatoes - boiled and peeled

MIX TOGETHER
1¼ cups curd
2 tsp cornflour, 3/4 tsp salt
¼ tsp kesar dissolved in 1 tbsp hot water
2 tbsp poodina (mint) chopped, 2 tbsp dhania (coriander) chopped

OTHER INGREDIENTS
1 tbsp oil
½ tsp shah jeera (black cumin), 1 moti illaichi (black cardamom), 2-3 laung (cloves)
1 onion - sliced
2 tbsp ginger-garlic paste
½ tsp red chilli powder, ¼ tsp haldi, ½ tsp salt
1 tsp dhania powder, ½ tsp garam masala
2 green chillies - slit deseeded & cut into thin long pieces
1 tomato - cut into wedges

1. Boil and peel potatoes. If the potatoes are the normal ones, cut them into four pieces. If using baby potatoes, keep them whole.
2. Beat curd to make it smooth. Add cornflour, salt, kesar, poodina and dhania to the whipped curd.
3. Heat oil in a fairly large kadhai. Add shah jeera, moti illaichi & laung. Wait for 1 minute.
4. Add onion. Stir fry till golden brown on low heat.
5. Add ginger-garlic paste. Mix.
6. Add red chilli powder, haldi, salt, garam masala & dhania powder.
7. Add potatoes and mix well. Keep them spaced out in the kadhai, do not overlap them. Stir very occasionally, scraping the masala which sticks to the bottom. Stir occasionally for 8-10 minutes till crisp.
8. Add the curd mix. Cook on low heat till the masala dries up and turns a little thick which coats the potatoes.
9. Add green chillies & tomato. Remove from fire. Serve.

Sukha Dahi Murg

cal/serving   149   *Serves 8*

1 chicken, approx. 800 gm - cut into pieces of your choice
2 capsicums - sliced thinly
2 cups skim milk curd, preferably 1 day old
1½ tsp salt, or to taste
1½ tsp black pepper, or to taste
1 small onion - grated or ground
1 tbsp oil

1. Beat curd well. Add salt, pepper and chicken. Let it marinate for 3-4 hours in the fridge.
2. Heat a non stick pan. Add oil, heat. Add ground onion. Cook till light brown.
3. Add chicken along with the marinade. Keep stirring till it boils.
4. Cover and lower heat. Cook till chicken turns tender, for about 7-8 minutes.
5. The curd being skim milk curd leaves a lot of water. When chicken tenders, increase heat and when nearly dry, add capsicum. Do not overcook capsicum. Cook for 1-2 minutes and serve hot.

Murg Kali Mirch

cal/serving   147   *Serves 8*

Freshly ground pepper from peppercorns, gives a better flavour.

1 chicken, approx. 800 gm - cut into pieces of your choice
(you can also use boneless chicken or chicken breasts)
1½ tsp black peppercorns - coarsely powdered, 1 tsp salt
juice of 2 large lemons (4-5 tbsp)
2 tsp oil

1. Heat oil in a non stick pan. Add chicken. Stir fry for 2-3 minutes.
2. Add salt and 1 tsp crushed peppercorns. Cover. Lower heat and cook till chicken is tender for about 7-8 minutes.
3. Increase heat. Add lemon juice. Cook till dry.
4. Serve hot garnished with lemon wedges and sprinkled with some more crushed peppercorns.

Saunf Waale Khatte Baingan

Picture on facing page   *Serves 3-4*   *cal/serving* 20

Delicious oil free brinjals. Brinjals cooked in water instead of oil!

250 gm small baingan (brinjals)
2 tsp imli (tamarind) pulp (pulp of a small marble sized ball of tamarind)
1 tsp sugar

DRY MASALAS
1 tsp salt
½ tsp red chilli
½ tsp haldi
1 tsp amchoor
½ tsp garam masala

DRY ROAST LIGHTLY AND POWDER
1 tbsp saunf (aniseeds)
2 tsp saboot dhania (coriander seeds)

1. Wash the brinjals and give 2 crosswise cuts from the top of the brinjals till half length, keeping the base intact.
2. Mix all the dry masalas. Add the roasted and ground saunf and dhania too. Mix 2 tsp of water with the masala to make it wet.
3. Fill the masala in brinjals properly.
4. In a non stick pan, add half cup water and the brinjals. Cook covered on low flame for 15-20 minutes till they turn soft, gently turning occasionally to cook the brinjals well from all sides. Cook till the water dries and the brinjals turn very soft.
5. Mix imli pulp with a little water and sugar. Add imli to the cooked brinjals. Stir for 2-3 minutes on fire.
6. Serve hot garnished with green chillies and onion rings.

Saunf Waale Khatte Baingan ➤

LOW FAT DISHES

FROM

FAR & WIDE

Szechwan Baby Corns

(Chinese)

cal/serving   42   Serves 4-6

Really low cal Chinese dish! Enjoy it with boiled rice.

200 gms baby corns - keep whole if small and divide into two lengthwise, if thick
3/4 cup water
1 seasoning cube
2 tbsp ginger-garlic paste
3-4 dry, red chillies
2 capsicums, (1 red or yellow and 1 green) - cut into 1" pieces
1 onion - cut into 4 pieces & separated
1½ tbsp soya sauce
2 tsp vinegar
3 tbsp tomato sauce
a pinch of ajinomoto
¼ tsp red chilli powder
1½ tbsp cornflour dissolved in ½ cup water

1. Mix water and seasoning cube in a pan. Add ginger-garlic paste and red chillies. Keep on fire and give one boil.
2. Add baby corns. Simmer on low flame for 5 minutes, till baby corns get done.
3. Mix cornflour in water. Add soya sauce, vinegar, tomato sauce, ajinomoto & red chilli powder. Add cornflour paste to the cooked baby corns.
4. Add capsicums and onions and cook further for 2 minutes till the sauce turns thick and coats the baby corns. Check salt (seasoning cube has salt) & add if required. Remove from fire and serve hot with noodles or rice.

Chicken Sizzler

Serves 4   *cal/serving 163*

4 chicken fillets (from 2 breast pieces)
1 tbsp oil

MARINADE
1½ tbsp vinegar
3 tbsp tomato ketchup, 1 tbsp worcestershire sauce
1 tsp mustard paste, ½ tsp salt, ½ tsp pepper

SAUCE
1 tsp garlic - chopped and crushed
1½ tbsp maida (plain flour)
3 tbsp tomato puree, 1 tsp worcestershire sauce, ½ tsp chilli powder
1 cube chicken super seasoning (optional)
1½ cups water, 1 tbsp oil

1. Marinate the chicken pieces with all the ingredients given under the marinade for 1-2 hours.
2. Heat 1 tbsp oil in a pressure cooker. Add the marinated chicken pieces and stir fry on high flame for 1 minute or till the chicken is dry.
3. Add 3/4 cup water and pressure cook to give 2 whistles. Immediately remove from fire to avoid the chicken getting over cooked.
4. After the pressure drops, check the chicken for tenderness. Return the cooker to heat. Stir for ½ minute. Remove the chicken pieces leaving behind the liquid. Remove from fire.
5. To the liquid in the cooker, add ½ cup water, tomato puree, worcestershire sauce, chicken cube and chilli powder.
6. Heat 1 tbsp oil in nonstick pan. Add garlic. Stir. Add maida. Stir on low flame for ½ minute. Add the retained liquid to which sauces are added, and cook stirring continuously till it turns a little thick. Remove from fire.
7. Remove the iron sizzler plate from the wooden base. Put 2-3 tbsp water in the wooden base. Heat the iron plate by keeping it directly on the flame. Heat till the plate gets really hot. Reduce heat.
8. Place 2-3 cabbage leaves on the sizzler plate and arrange chicken fillet on it. Pour the hot sauce over it. Arrange boiled vegetables on it.
9. Dot the iron plate with butter. Remove from fire with the help of a firm pair of tongs (sansi), place it on the wooden tray which has a little water in it. Serve sizzling hot.

Hot & Sour Cabbage

(Chinese)

cal/serving 46   Serves 4

A quick preparation, which lends colour to the table spread. An interesting side dish too!

1 small green cabbage or ½ red & ½ green cabbage (mixed) - shredded (2½ cups)
1 carrot - cut into thin juliennes (½ cup)
2 green chillies - cut into thin long strips
1 capsicum - deseeded and shredded
1 tbsp oil
¼ tsp ajinomoto - optional
¼ tsp pepper, ¼ tsp sugar
½ tsp salt or to taste
¼ tsp red chilli powder

SAUCE (MIX TOGETHER)
½ cup water
1 level tbsp cornflour
1 tbsp soya sauce
1½ tbsp vinegar
1½ tbsp tomato ketchup

1. To cut carrot, peel carrot. Cut whole carrot lengthwise into thin, flat slices. Cut each slice into thin match sticks.
2. Shred all the other vegetables also into thin long strips.
3. Heat oil in a large woke or a non-stick kadhai. Add carrots, cook for 1 minute.
4. Add cabbage, capsicum and green chillies. Mix well.
5. Add salt, pepper, sugar and ajinomoto. Stir fry for 2 minutes on medium flame.
6. Add all the ingredients mixed together for the sauce. Stir fry on low flame for 2 minutes till almost dry, but not completely dry.
7. Serve hot, sprinkled with a little red chilli powder, if you like it really hot.

Stroganoff Chicken

(Continental)

Serves 8   *cal/serving*   176

Delicious low calorie creamy chicken without any cream.

1 chicken (approx. 1 kg) - cut into bite size pieces
200 gms mushrooms - sliced
2 tsp oil, 1 onion - chopped fine
1 cup low fat curd (made from low fat milk), 2 tbsp maida
1¼ tsp salt, ½-1 tsp red chilli powder

1. Heat 2 tsp oil in a nonstick pan. Add onion and saute for 1-2 minutes.
2. Add chicken, salt and red chilli powder. Fry on high heat for 2-3 minutes.
3. Lower heat. Cook covered for 5-6 minutes or till chicken is nearly tender.
4. Add mushrooms. Cook covered on low heat for another 4-5 minutes.
5. Mix maida to curd and mix well so that no lumps remain.
6. Add to the chicken. Cook uncovered till sauce thickens. Serve hot sprinkled with fresh coriander leaves.

Mediterranean Chicken

Serves 2-3   *cal/serving*   150

Makes a delicious full meal as spaghetti is served along with the chicken.

250 gms chicken, 2 tsp oil
2 flakes garlic - crushed, 3 large tomatoes - pureed in mixer
¼ cup wine (optional)
1 tej patta (bay leaf), 1 tsp dried basil
1 tsp sugar, 3/4 tsp salt (adjust to taste)
3/4 tsp red chilli powder (adjust to taste)
1 tbsp cornflour
100 gms boiled spaghetti - to serve

1. Heat oil in a nonstick pan. Add chicken and cook till dry and changes colour.
2. Add tomatoes and all the other ingredients, except cornflour.
3. Cover and simmer for 7-8 minutes or till chicken is tender.
4. Dissolve cornflour in 1 tbsp water and add to the chicken.
5. Boil well and serve over boiled spaghetti.

Spicy Honeyed Veggies

(Chinese)

cal/serving 99   *Serves 4*

**1 small carrot - parboiled and cut into flowers or round slices
½ cup cauliflower or broccoli - cut into small, flat florets (¼ of a small flower)
4-5 mushrooms - trim stalks and keep whole if small or cut into 2 pieces
4-6 baby corns (optional) - keep whole if small or divide into 2 lengthwise, if thick
1 capsicum - cut into ½" cubes, 1 small onion - cut into 4 pieces and separated
2 tbsp cornflour dissolved in ½ cup water with 1 seasoning cube
2 tbsp oil
3-4 dry, red chillies - broken into bits, 8-10 flakes garlic - crushed
¼ tsp each - salt and pepper, or to taste
a pinch ajinomoto, ¼ tsp red chilli powder
½ tbsp vinegar, 1 tbsp soya sauce, 1½ tbsp tomato sauce
2 tsp chilli sauce, 2-3 tsp honey**

TO SERVE
4 cups boiled rice

1. Break cauliflower or broccoli into small florets and cut each floret into two. Trim mushrooms and baby corns, keeping them whole. Peel carrots.
2. Boil 4 cups water with 1 tsp salt. Drop the whole carrot, mushrooms, baby corns and florets of cauliflower in boiling water. Let it boil for 2 minutes. Remove from water. Refresh veggies in cold water.
3. Cut parboiled carrot into ¼" thick round slices or flowers. Cut capsicum into ½" pieces. Cut onion into fours and separate the slices.
4. Dissolve cornflour in ½ cup water. Add seasoning cube and keep aside.
5. Heat oil in a kadhai. Reduce heat and add broken red chillies and garlic.
6. Stir and add baby corns, carrots, cauliflower, mushrooms and onions. Stir for 2-3 minutes or till veggies are done. Add capsicum. Add salt & pepper. Add a pinch of ajinomoto & ¼ tsp red chilli powder.
7. Stir and add chilli sauce, tomato sauce, soya sauce, honey and vinegar. Lower heat and stir for ½ minute.
8. Add the dissolved cornflour and seasoning cube. Cook till the vegetables get done and are crisp tender, and the sauce coats the veggies.
9. Spread the warm rice in a serving plate. Pour the hot vegetables over the rice and serve immediately.

Quick Chilli Chicken

(Chinese)

Serves 4-6   *cal/serving   180*

A fast, Chinese style of preparing dry, chilli chicken.

1 chicken (700-800 gms) - cut into small pieces
OR
500 gm boneless chicken
3 tbsp soya sauce
½ tsp pepper powder, ½ tsp salt
½ tsp sugar
¼ tsp ajinomoto (optional)
2 tbsp oil

GRIND TOGETHER
2-3 dry red chillies - soaked in 1½ tbsp vinegar for 10 minutes
15 flakes garlic
1" piece ginger

GARNISH
6-8 green chillies - slit lengthwise
1-2 spring onion greens - cut into ½" pieces
1 capsicum - cut into ½" pieces

1. Cut the chicken into small pieces by placing a sharp knife over the piece and hitting the knife with anything hard that cracks the bone and can cut through the piece, or take boneless chicken and cut into 2" pieces.
2. Grind together red chillies, ginger and garlic to get about 2 tbsp paste.
3. Marinate chicken with this paste, soya sauce, pepper, salt, sugar and ajinomoto for ½ hour.
3. Heat 2 tbsp oil in a pressure cooker, add the marinated chicken. Stir fry on high flame till the chicken is dry.
4. Add ½ cup water and close the lid of the pressure cooker. Pressure cook to give 1 whistle. Remove from flame, drop the pressure of the cooker by putting cold water on the lid and open.
5. Dry the chicken pieces on high flame.
6. Add green chillies, spring onion greens and capsicum. Stir well and serve hot.

Thai Green Curry
with Paneer & Aubergines

Picture on cover   *Serves 4*   *cal/serving* 119

100 gms paneer - cut into 1" cubes
2- 3 small aubergines (brinjals) - cut into very thin slices
1 tbsp oil
2½ cups coconut milk or use one packet coconut powder (maggie) mixed with
1½ cups milk and 1 cup water, 1 tsp sugar or gur
1 tsp salt
½ tsp dried basil (dried tulsi leaves)
3 tbsp chopped fresh basil (tulsi) or coriander leaves
2-3 green or red chillies - slit long for garnishing

GREEN CURRY PASTE
6-7 green chillies, ½ onion - chopped
1 tbsp chopped garlic, ½" piece ginger - chopped
1 stick lemon grass (use only the lower portion) - cut into pieces, discard the leaves
2-3 lemon leaves, see note (nimbu ke patte) or ½ tsp lemon rind
4 tbsp coriander leaves
½ tsp salt, 15 peppercorns (saboot kali mirch)
1 tbsp white vinegar
1 tbsp coriander seeds (saboot dhania)
1 tbsp jeera (cumin seeds)

1. For the green curry paste, dry roast coriander and cumin seeds for 2 minutes on a tawa till fragrant but not brown. Put all other ingredients of the curry paste and the roasted seeds in a grinder and grind to a fine paste, using a little water.
2. Heat oil in a kadhai. Add green curry paste. Fry for 2-3 minutes.
3. Add 1 cup coconut milk. Simmer on low heat for 5-7 minutes.
4. Add salt, sugar, basil, brinjals and the rest of coconut milk. Boil. Cover and cook on low heat for about 5 minutes or till brinjals are well cooked.
5. Add paneer. Give 2-3 boils.
6. Garnish with sliced red or green chillies (long thin slices), basil leaves.
7. Serve hot with boiled/steamed rice.

Note: Discard 1" from the bottom of the lemon grass. Peel a few outer leaves. Chop into ½" pieces until the stem. Discard the upper grass like portion.

Thai Fish Curry

Picture on facing page   *Serves 6*   *cal/serving* 213

600 gms fish - cleaned & washed and cut into small (3/4") pieces
2 tbsp oil
3 cups coconut milk extracted from 1 coconut or 3 cups ready made coconut milk
1 tbsp fish sauce
3-4 lemon leaves
1 tsp salt, 2 tsp sugar/gur (optional)
½ cup basil leaves - shredded, 3-4 chillies (green or red) - sliced

RED CURRY PASTE
2 dry, Kashmiri red chillies - soaked in ¼ cup warm water for 10 minutes
½ of a small onion - chopped, 4-5 flakes garlic - peeled, ½" piece ginger - sliced
1 stalk lemon grass or rind of 1 lemon, 1 stalks coriander
3/4 tsp coriander seeds (dhania saboot), ½ tsp cumin (jeera)
2-3 peppercorns (saboot kali mirch), ½ tsp salt, ½ tbsp vinegar

1. Grind all the ingredients of the red curry paste along with the water in which the chillies were soaked, to a very fine paste.
2. Extract 3 cups of coconut milk by soaking freshly grated coconut in 1 cup of warm water for 20 minutes. Blend and then squeeze through a muslin cloth. To the left over residue of the coconut in the cloth add 2 more cups hot water and soak it for 10 minutes. Squeeze again through a muslin to get more milk (3 cups in all).
3. Heat oil. Add curry paste. Fry for 2 minutes on low heat.
4. Add ½ cup coconut milk. Cook till nearly dry and fragrant.
5. Add fish sauce, lemon leaves, salt and sugar. Add the rest of the coconut milk. Add 1 cup water. Give it one boil.
6. Add fish and basil. Cover and cook for 5-6 minutes, till fish is well done.
7. Garnish with sliced chillies and serve hot with steamed/boiled rice.

Note: Instead of fish, prawns, crabs, paneer and mixed vegetables can be used.

Thai Fish Curry ➢

Basil & Tomato Pasta

(Italian)

Serves 4-6   *cal/serving* 86

SAUCE
1 tbsp olive oil or any cooking oil
1 onion - finely chopped
8-10 garlic flakes - chopped
500 gm (6-7) tomatoes - blanched in hot water, skinned & chopped finely
1 tsp dried oregano
1 tbsp tomato ketchup, 1 tbsp tomato puree
½ tsp sugar
½ tsp red chilli flakes or powder, 1 tsp salt, or to taste
2 tbsp chopped fresh basil (or tulsi, holy basil)

PASTA
1 tbsp olive oil or butter
2 cups penne or any other pasta - boiled to get 3 cups cooked pasta
½ tsp salt, ½ tsp peppercorns - crushed, ½ tsp oregano

OTHER INGREDIENTS
2 tbsp grated cheese (mozzarella or parmesan) to sprinkle on top, optional
a few basil leaves - put in chilled water to garnish

1. To boil pasta, boil 8-10 cups water with 2 tsp salt. Add pasta to boiling water and stir. Cook on high heat, stirring in-between gently (pasta sticks to the bottom) for 7-8 minutes or till almost tender. Do not overcook. Remove from fire. Leave it in hot water for just 2-3 minutes till done. Drain the water. Add fresh cold water and strain and keep aside.
2. To prepare the sauce, heat oil. Add onion & garlic, stir fry until onions turn light brown.
3. Add tomatoes, oregano, tomato ketchup, tomato puree, red chilli powder, salt and sugar, cook for 5 minutes, stirring occasionally. Remove from fire. Add fresh basil. Keep sauce aside.
4. At serving time, melt 1 tbsp olive oil or butter in a non stick pan and toss the pasta in it. Sprinkle some salt, some freshly crushed pepper and oregano on it. Mix gently till it's heated. Remove from fire.
5. Heat tomato sauce. Add pasta and heat through. Transfer to a serving dish.
6. Serve sprinkled with grated cheese and basil leaves.

Bean Burritos

(A Complete Mexican Meal)

cal/serving 239   *Serves 6-8*

BEAN FILLING
3/4 cup red rajmah (kidney beans) - soaked overnight or for 5-6 hours
3/4 tsp salt, 1 dry, red chilli
1 tbsp oil, 1 onion - finely chopped, 2 flakes garlic - finely chopped

DOUGH
1 cup maida (plain flour), 1 cup atta (wheat flour), ¼ tsp salt, 1 tbsp oil

HOT SAUCE
3 dry red chillies - soaked in ¼ cup water, 5 red tomatoes - skinned & chopped
1 tbsp oil, ½ tsp ajwain, 3-4 flakes garlic - minced, 2 onions - chopped finely
3/4 tsp salt & ½ tsp pepper, 2 tbsp tomato sauce

LOW FAT SOUR CREAM
3/4 cup thick curd - hung for ½ hour in a thin cloth
½ tsp salt, few drops tabasco sauce, a few spring onion greens for garnish

1. Boil or pressure cook soaked rajmah along with salt and a dry red chilli.
2. To prepare the dough, sieve maida & atta. Add salt and oil. Knead to a soft dough with warm water. Cover and keep aside.
3. For the sauce, soak dry red chillies in ¼ cup warm water for 15 minutes.
4. Dip tomatoes in hot water for 10 min. Remove skin. Chop finely. Mash chillies.
5. To prepare the sauce, heat oil. Add ajwain. Add garlic & onions. Fry till onions turn transparent. Add tomatoes and mashed red chillies along with the water. Cook till tomatoes turn pulpy. Mash well. Add salt, pepper and 2 tbsp tomato sauce. Cook for 7-10 minutes. Keep the hot sauce aside.
6. To prepare the filling, heat oil. Cook onions and garlic till pink. Add boiled rajmah, 2 tbsp of the prepared hot sauce and salt. Cook for 5 minutes. Remove from fire and mash coarsely.
7. For the sour cream, beat hung curd well till smooth. Add salt and tabasco sauce.
8. Make 8 small balls of the prepared dough. Roll out into very thin chappatis.
9. Cook the chappatis on a tawa. Keep the cooked chappatis soft in a casserole.
10. At the time of serving, heat the rajmah filling, spread little filling on the chappati. Pour a little hot sauce & then sour cream over the rajmah.
11. Fold sides. Roll up. Fry in 1 tbsp oil in a non-stick pan or a tawa till crisp. Serve hot topped with some hot sauce, sour cream & spring onion greens.

Thai Red Curry with Vegetables

Picture on page 99   *Serves 4-6*   *cal/serving 72*

A spicy red curry simmered with assorted vegetables. Enjoy it with noodles or boiled rice.

RED CURRY PASTE

4-5 dry, Kashmiri red chillies - soaked in ½ cup warm water for 10 minutes
½ onion - chopped
8-10 flakes garlic - peeled
1½" piece ginger - sliced
1 stalk lemon grass or rind of 1 lemon
3 stalks coriander
1½ tsp coriander seeds (dhania saboot), 1 tsp cumin (jeera)
6 peppercorns (saboot kali mirch), 1 tsp salt, 1 tbsp vinegar

VEGETABLES

6-8 baby corns - slit lengthwise
2 small brinjals - peeled and diced into ½" pieces (small)
1 small broccoli - cut into florets, 5-6 mushrooms - sliced
¼ cup chopped bamboo shoots (optional)

OTHER INGREDIENTS

3 cups coconut milk exctracted from one grated coconut OR use one packet
coconut powder (maggie) mixed with 2 cups milk and 1 cup water
1 tbsp cornflour, ½ tsp soya sauce
15- 20 basil leaves (tulsi) - chopped or some coriander leaves
salt to taste, ½ tsp brown sugar

1. Grind all the ingredients of the red curry paste along with the water in which the chillies were soaked, to a very fine paste.
2. Extract 3 cups of coconut milk by soaking grated coconut in 1 cup of warm water for 20 minutes. Blend and then squeeze through a muslin cloth. To the left over residue of the coconut in the cloth add 2 more cups hot water and soak it for 10 minutes. Squeeze again through a muslin to get more milk (3 cups).
3. Add the red curry paste in a non stick pan and fry for a few seconds on low heat.
4. Add 3- 4 tbsp of coconut milk. Add vegetables and cook for 2-3 minutes.
5. Add the rest of the coconut milk, soya sauce and chopped basil leaves.
6. Cover and simmer on low heat for 5-7 minutes till the vegetables are tender.
7. Add salt and sugar to taste. Boil for 1 to 2 minutes. Serve hot with steamed rice.

Chicken in Red Curry

You can use 500 gm boneless chicken instead of vegetables.

Chicken Fiesta

(Italian)

cal/serving 155   *Serves 8*

A delicious tomato flavoured chicken with contrasting white and green rice.

1 chicken (approx. 500 gm) - cut into pieces of your choice
1 tbsp oil
4 large tomatoes - pureed in the mixer
3-4 flakes garlic - crushed
1 tbsp kishmish (raisins)
3-4 spring onions or ½ cup onions chopped finely
1 tsp dried oregano
1 tsp red chilli flakes or powder, or to taste
1½ tsp salt, or to taste
1 tsp sugar

OTHER INGREDIENTS
a pinch of orange red colour
1½-2 tbsp cornflour

TO SERVE
1 cup boiled rice mixed with ¼ cup finely chopped fresh coriander or parsley

1. In a nonstick pan, heat oil. Stir fry chicken for 3-4 minutes. Reduce heat.
2. Add pureed tomatoes, crushed garlic, raisins, onion, oregano, red chilli flakes, salt and sugar. Give one boil. Cover and cook till chicken turns tender.
3. Dissolve cornflour in 1-2 tbsp water. Add colour to it.
4. Add to the chicken. Boil. Cook till sauce turns thick.
5. For serving the chicken, boil rice and remove excess water, so that the starch is removed. Keep chicken aside.
6. Toss the boiled rice with chopped parsley or coriander.
7. Serve chicken with rice.

Chicken Steak

(Continental)

Serves 4   cal/serving   176

Succulent steaks of chicken mince.

STEAK
½ kg chicken mince (keema)
2 medium onions - chopped finely, 2" piece ginger - chopped
½ cup green coriander chopped, 2 green chillies - chopped
2 tbsp worcestershire sauce, 2 tbsp tomato ketchup
1 egg white, 2 tbsp maida
1 tsp mustard powder, salt & pepper to taste
1 slice fresh bread - dipped in water, squeezed & crumbled
1 tbsp oil

GARLIC SAUCE
1 tsp oil
8-10 flakes garlic - chopped & crushed
1 tbsp worcestershire sauce, 1 tsp 8-8 sauce, 2 tbsp tomato ketchup
¼ tsp pepper, ¼ tsp salt or to taste
1 tbsp cornflour mixed with ¼ cup water

1. Wash and strain the mince. Squeeze out all the water by pressing the mince well in the strainer. The mince should be absolutely dry.
2. Add all the other ingredients given under steak, to the drained mince. Knead the mince well to mix all the ingredients. Keep aside for ½ hour as the salt and ginger act as tenderizers.
3. Make 8 flat round steaks (tikkis) of mince. Refrigerate for ½ hour. Heat a non stick tawa with 1 tbsp oil. Fry steaks on high heat to brown both sides. Reduce flame and fry on low flame till well cooked.
4. To prepare garlic sauce, heat 1 tsp oil. Add garlic paste and stir fry on low flame till it changes colour. Add all the 3 sauces, salt & pepper.
5. Stir. Add 3/4 cup water. Boil. Add cornflour paste, stirring continuously. Cook till sauce thickens. Keep aside.
6. To serve, place the steaks in a serving plate. Pour some hot garlic sauce over them and serve accompanied with some boiled vegetables (small cauliflower florets, 1" pieces of beans, round slices of carrot etc.).

From the Oven
BAKED, TANDOORI, GRILLED

Tandoori Paneer with Capsicum

Serves 4   cal/serving   136

A delightful paneer dish.

250 gms paneer (prepared from skim milk) - cut into 1" cubes
3/4 tsp salt
¼ tsp red chilli powder
¼ tsp haldi (turmeric powder) or a pinch of red colour
1 tsp lemon juice
1 tbsp oil
2 capsicums - cut into fine rings
2 onions - cut into fine rings
¼ tsp kaala namak (black salt), ¼ tsp salt
2 tsp tandoori masala

GRIND TO A ROUGH PASTE
1½" piece ginger
2-3 green chillies
1 tsp jeera (cumin seeds)
3-4 flakes garlic - optional

1. Grind garlic, ginger, jeera & green chillies to a thick rough paste. Do not add water.
2. Add salt, chilli powder and lemon juice to the paste. Add a little haldi or colour to give colour to the paste.
3. Cut paneer into 1" squares. Apply 3/4 of this paste nicely on all the pieces. Keep the left over paste aside.
4. Grill this paneer on a greased wire rack and grill for 10 minutes till it is dry and slightly crisp. Keep aside till serving time.
5. At serving time, heat 1 tbsp oil in a kadhai. Fry onion & capsicum rings for a few minutes till onions turn transparent. Keep aside a few capsicum rings for garnishing.
6. Add the ginger paste and few drops of lemon juice. Add black salt and little salt too.
7. Add paneer pieces. Sprinkle tandoori masala. Toss for a minutes till the paneer turns soft and is heated properly.
8. Serve immediately, garnished with the capsicum rings kept aside.

Mixed Greens Baked with Corn

cal/serving 104   *Serves 6*

A very healthy baked dish with mixed greens topped with soft and crunchy corn.

1 cup spinach - shredded
1 cup cabbage - shredded
1 cup broccoli - finely chopped (finely chop 1" of the stalks also below the florets)
½ cup boiled or tinned corn kernels
½ tsp red chilli flakes
4-5 flakes garlic - crushed
1 onion - thinly sliced
8-10 peppercorns - crushed coarsely
1 tbsp oil
1 tomato - cut into slices

SAUCE
1½ tbsp oil
2 tbsp maida (plain flour)
1½ cups milk
1 tsp salt and ½ tsp pepper, or to taste

1. Boil water in a large pan with 1 tsp salt. Add broccoli to boiling water. As soon as the boil returns, add other greens. When the boil comes again remove from fire. Strain well to drain water.
2. Heat 1 tbsp oil. Saute garlic and onion till onion turns transparent.
3. Add half of the crushed peppercorns and ½ tsp salt.
4. Squeeze greens gently and add to the onions. Cook till dry on low flame for 3-4 minutes. Remove from fire.
5. To prepare the sauce, heat oil. Reduce heat and add flour. Cook for 1 minute. Add milk, stirring continuously. Stir on medium flame till a sauce of medium thick consistency is obtained. Add salt and pepper to taste. Keep aside.
6. In a dish arrange the greens 1½ - 2" thick layer.
7. Spread cooked corn (not too much) on it.
8. Sprinkle some red chilli flakes.
9. Pour the prepared sauce to cover well.
10. Arrange overlapping slices of tomatoes on it. Sprinkle some crushed peppercorns.
11. Bake at 200°C for 25-30 minutes or till golden.

Chicken Grilled with Orange Juice

Picture on facing page　　　　　*Serves 2*　　　　　*cal/serving*　160

300 gms chicken (1 leg and 1 breast piece)
3 tbsp lemon juice
½ cup fresh orange juice
4-6 cloves garlic - chopped fine or minced
1 tsp tabasco or chilli sauce
1 tbsp chopped fresh coriander
1 tsp salt
3/4 tsp coarsely ground peppercorns
1 tsp cornflour

1. Wash and pat dry the chicken pieces on a kitchen towel. Make 2 incisions on each piece.
2. Mix all ingredients except cornflour. Marinate chicken for 6-8 hours turning over chicken pieces 2-3 times.
3. Heat grill. Remove chicken pieces from marinade. Sprinkle some more pepper on top and grill for 10-12 minutes or till chicken is well cooked and crisp. Baste inbetween with the marinade to prevent the chicken from turning dry. (Alternately cook in the oven for 15-20 minutes or on a greased non stick pan. In the pan, cover the chicken and after it is cooked increase heat to dry all water and cook it crisp).
4. Place chicken pieces on a serving dish.
5. Mix cornflour to the remaining marinade.
6. Give 1-2 boils. Pour over the prepared chicken and serve hot along with some steamed vegetables.

Chicken Grilled with Orange Juice ➤

Layered Masala Paneer

Servings 6   *cal/serving*   155

An attractive paneer dish with three different fillings, each imparting it's own flavour.

½ kg paneer (cottage cheese) - brick shape, pat dry on a clean tissue
¼ cup boiled peas - to garnish

GREEN FILLING
1 small bunch coriander, 1 green chilli, 1 small onion, salt to taste
½ tsp amchoor (dried mango powder)

DRY MASALA FILLING
½ tsp salt, ½ tsp red chilli powder, ½ tsp amchoor, ½ tsp crushed bhuna jeera
2 tsp crushed kasoori methi

TOMATO FILLING
2 tomatoes - roughly chopped, 2-3 flakes garlic, ½" piece ginger - chopped
2 tbsp tomato ketchup, 1/3 tsp peppercorns - crushed, 1/3 tsp salt, or to taste

GRAVY
2 onions, 4 flakes garlic, 1" piece ginger - paste
2 tomatoes - blanched (skin removed) and chopped
1 tbsp oil, ½ tsp jeera (cumin seeds), 2 tbsp chopped coriander
½ tsp salt, ½ tsp chilli powder, ¼ tsp haldi, ¼ tsp amchoor, ¼ tsp garam masala

1. Grind all ingredients of the green filling together to a thick rough paste.
2. Mix all powders of the dry filling. Keep aside.
3. For tomato filling, blend tomatoes, garlic & ginger in a mixer. Keep on fire. Add ketchup, salt & peppercorns and cook for 5 minutes on medium flame till thick.
4. To prepare the gravy, grind onions, ginger and garlic together to a paste.
5. Heat oil in a nonstick pan. Add jeera. When jeera turns golden, add onion paste. Fry till light brown. Add haldi and chilli powder. Cook for ½ minute. Add tomatoes. Cook for 3-4 minutes. Add ½ cup water and coriander to get a thick masala gravy. Add salt and garam masala. Boil for 2-3 minutes. Keep gravy aside.
6. To assemble, pat dry paneer on a tissue to absorb any water. Cut paneer into 4 slices, horizontally. In an oven-proof rectangular dish arrange a slice. Spread some green filling generously on it. Press gently. Put the second paneer piece over the first. Sprinkle all the dry masala over the paneer. Cover it with the third paneer piece. Spread tomato filling. Cover with the last piece of paneer. Press.
7. Top the brick with gravy and let the gravy fall on the sides in the dish also. Garnish with boiled peas. Cover the dish loosely with a foil and keep aside. At serving time, heat in an oven at 180°C for 25-30 minutes or heat well in a microwave covered with a cling film. Serve hot.

Tandoori Chicken

cal/serving 167   *Serves 6*

1 medium sized chicken (800 gm) - cut into 6-8 pieces
juice of 1 lemon
1 tsp chilli powder, salt to taste

MARINADE
1 cup curd - hung for 30 minutes or more
2 tsp kasoori methi (dry fenugreek leaves)
10-15 flakes garlic and 1½" ginger - crushed to a paste or 2 tbsp ginger-garlic paste
½ tsp kala namak
½ tsp garam masala
2 tsp tandoori masala
few drops orange red colour
1 tsp cornflour

OTHER INGREDIENTS
2 tsp oil to baste chicken while grilling
lemon wedges and onion rings

1. Wash, pat dry chicken. Make 2 incisions on the breast, 2 on each thigh & 2 on each drumstick.
2. Rub lemon juice, salt & chilli powder on the chicken & keep aside for ½ hour.
3. For the marinade, mix hung curd, kasoori methi, garlic & ginger paste, kala namak, garam masala, tandoori masala and colour. Add cornflour and mix well. Rub the chicken with this marinade. Keep aside for 3-4 hours in the fridge.
4. Heat the gas tandoor (flame should be minimum) or oven to 180°C. Place the chicken on the grill or wire rack (in the oven place a tray underneath the chicken to collect the drippings).
5. Grill for 15 minutes. Brush or sprinkle oil on the chicken pieces. Turn pieces & grill for another 10-15 minutes, till the chicken is dry and well cooked. Be careful not to make the chicken blackish and burnt.
6. Sprinkle some kasoori methi. Serve hot with lemon wedges and onion rings.

Ajwaini Mushrooms in Tomato Cups

Serves 8   *cal/serving*   50

8 firm medium size tomatoes
200 gm mushrooms - finely chopped, chop the stalks also
2 spring onions - finely chopped upto the greens, keep greens separate
50 gm (½ cup) grated or roughly mashed paneer
1 tsp very finely chopped ginger
1 tsp lemon juice
1 tbsp oil or butter
½ tsp ajwain
3/4 tsp salt and ¼ tsp red chilli powder, or to taste
2 laung (cloves) - crushed to a powder
a few coriander leaves dipped in chilled water for ½ hour
a few lettuce or cabbage leaves

1. Slice ¼" thick slice from the top of the tomatoes. Scoop out the pulp with the help of the back of a small spoon from tomatoes. See if the tomato sits on the plate easily, otherwise slice a little from the bottom to make it even and sit properly.

2. Rub the inner surface of the tomatoes with salt. Rub some salt on the outer surface too. Keep the tomatoes upside down.

3. Heat oil or butter. Add ajwain and wait for a minute. Add the white part of onions. Saute for 1-2 minutes till soft.

4. Add mushrooms and stir fry for 5-6 minutes, till mushrooms become dry and turn light brown.

5. Reduce flame. Add salt, chilli powder and powdered laung. Add the greens of spring onions. Mix and remove from fire.

6. Add paneer, ginger and lemon juice. Mix gently. Remove from fire. Check seasonings. Cool.

7. Fill the tomato scoops with the mushroom mixture. Press gently.

8. Place on a greased tray and bake for 9-10 minutes in a hot oven at 220°C. Do not over bake as they turn limp.

9. Remove from oven and arrange a coriander leaf on each baked tomato. Serve on a bed of cabbage or lettuce leaves.

Red-Green-White Casserole

cal/serving   48   *Serves 4-5*

RED LAYER
½ tin (1 cup) baked beans, see note

GREEN LAYER
2 cups finely chopped spinach

WHITE
250 gms paneer - crumbled roughly
1 tsp salt, ½ tsp pepper
1-2 tsp milk

FAT FREE WHITE SAUCE
1 cup milk
1 small onion - very finely chopped
2 green chillies - very finely chopped
2-3 garlic flakes - crushed or ¼ tsp garlic paste
1 tbsp cornflour
½ tsp salt, or to taste
½ tsp oregano

1. Finely chop spinach and boil in ½ cup water and ¼ tsp salt for 5 minutes. Strain and squeeze to remove any extra water.
2. Crumble the paneer. Add 1 tsp salt & ½ tsp pepper, or to taste. Keep aside.
3. Prepare the white sauce by mixing all the ingredients together. Keep on fire in a heavy bottomed kadhai. Cook, stirring continuously till you get a sauce of a thick pouring consistency.
4. In a lightly greased dish arrange the boiled spinach layer at the bottom. (½" thick).
5. On the palak layer spread the paneer layer, if the paneer is very dry, sprinkle 1-2 tsp of milk on it.
6. Spread the baked beans on the spinach-paneer layer.
7. Pour the white sauce in the centre over the baked beans, leaving the beans on the sides to show.
8. Bake for 15-20 minutes at 200°C till the white sauce turns light brown. Serve.

Note: Transfer the left over baked beans in a stainless steel box and keep in the freezer compartment of the refrigerator for a month or even more without getting spoilt.

Oven Fried Fish

Serves 4-5   *cal/serving*   132

Low cholesterol dish with no oil. Although called fried, it is in fact baked.

500 gms fish, preferably fillet - cut into 2" pieces to get 8-9 pieces
3/4 cup bread crumbs
1 tsp salt (adjust to taste)
1 tsp pepper (adjust to taste)
1 tsp amchoor (adjust to taste)
1 egg white, ¼ tsp salt and ¼ tsp pepper
1 tsp oil for greasing

1. Wash and dry fish on paper towels.
2. Sprinkle salt, pepper and amchoor on fish and mix well. Leave for 5 minutes.
3. Beat egg white lightly with ¼ tsp each of salt and pepper.
4. Dip fish pieces one by one in egg white and coat well with bread crumbs spread out in a plate.
5. Place on a greased tray and bake in a preheated oven at 230°C for 10 minutes.

Note:
- Time of baking will depend on the thickness of the fish.
- Chicken can also be made in the same way.

Herbed Baked Fish

Serves 2-3   *cal/serving*   113

350 gms fish - cut into 2" pieces
1 tsp oregano
1-2 tbsp finely chopped fresh parsley
½ tsp black peppercorns - crushed roughly
3 tbsp lemon juice
2 tbsp worcestershire sauce, 3/4 tsp salt (adjust to taste)
3-4 flakes garlic - chopped and crushed

1. Give cuts on each fish piece so that the marinade can penetrate well.
2. Mix everything together and let the fish marinate in it for 3-4 hours in the refrigerator.
3. Place on a greased tray and bake in a hot oven at 220°C for 25-30 minutes.

Note: The fish used should preferably be without skin and non-oily.

Fish Tikka

cal/serving 62 　　　　　　Serves 8 　　　　　　*Picture on page 2*

500 gm boneless Singhara or Sole fish - cut into 2" cubes

1ST MARINADE
2 tbsp vinegar or lemon juice
¼ tsp red chilli powder
½ tsp salt

2ND MARINADE
½ cup curd - hang for 30 minutes in a thin cloth
1 tbsp roughly crushed ginger-garlic paste (crush 10 flakes garlic and 1 " piece ginger together)
½ tsp garam masala powder
½ tsp ajwain (carom seeds)
3/4 tsp salt & ½ tsp chilli powder, or to taste
a pinch of orange colour or ¼ tsp haldi

GARNISHING
lemon wedges, mint or coriander sprigs, some chaat masala
juice of 1 lemon and tandoori masala to sprinkle

1. Wash and pat dry the tikka pieces on a tissue napkin or a kitchen towel.
2. Marinate fish with lemon juice, salt and red chilli powder. Keep aside for ½ hour.
3. In a bowl mix curd, ginger-garlic paste, garam masala, ajwain and little salt & pepper.
4. Add tikka pieces and coat well with this marinade. Keep in the refrigerator to marinate for 3-4 hours.
5. Heat a gas tandoor on gas or an electric oven at 200°C.
6. Skewer tikkas or place them on the grill and roast till coating turns dry and golden brown. Baste with a little oil in between.
7. Serve hot sprinkled with lemon juice and tandoori masala. Garnish the platter with lemon wedges and coriander.

Tandoori Bharwaan Aloo

Serves 6   *cal/serving   74*

3 big (longish) potatoes
1 tbsp til (sesame seeds), some chaat masala to sprinkle

FILLING
3 almonds - blanched & chopped very finely
4 tbsp grated paneer (50 gm)
1 tbsp poodina (mint) leaves - chopped, 1 green chilli - deseeded and chopped
¼ tsp garam masala, ¼ tsp red chilli powder, ¼ tsp salt, ¼ tsp amchoor

COVERING
½ cup thick curd - hung in a muslin cloth for 30 minutes
1" piece ginger - chopped finely and crushed coarsely
¼ tsp red chilli powder, ¾ tsp salt, ¼ tsp haldi or orange colour

CRUSH TOGETHER TO A ROUGH POWDER
1 tsp shah jeera (black cumin), seeds of 2 moti illaichi (brown cardamom)
2-3 blades of javitri (mace), 6-8 saboot kali mirch (peppercorns)

1. Boil potatoes in salted water till just tender. When they cool, peel skin.
2. Blanch almonds (remove skin by soaking in hot water) and chop them very finely. Mix almonds with mint leaves, green chillies, 4 tbsp grated paneer, ¼ tsp salt, ¼ tsp garam masala, ¼ tsp red chilli and a pinch of amchoor.
3. Grind or crush kala jeera, seeds of moti illaichi, peppercorns, and 2-3 pinches of javitri to a coarse powder.
4. To the almond-paneer paste, add ¼-½ teaspoon of the above freshly ground powder also. Keep the leftover powder aside.
5. Mix hung curd, ginger paste, the left over freshly ground powder and red chilli powder and salt. Add haldi or orange colour.
6. Peel potatoes. Run the tip of a fork on the surface of the potatoes, making the surface rough. (The rough surface holds the masalas well).
7. Cut each potato into 2 halves, vertically.
8. Scoop out, just a little, to get a small cavity in each potato with the back of a teaspoon. Put a little almond-paneer filling in each piece.
9. With a spoon apply the curd mixture on the outside of the potatoes and on the rim also (not on the filling). Sprinkle some sesame or til seeds.
10. Grill potatoes in a gas tandoor or a preheated oven at 210°C/410°F for 25 minutes on a greased wire rack till they get slightly charred and the coating turns absolutely dry. Sprinkle some chaat masala and serve with onion, kheera and tomato slices.

Baked Chicken with Spinach

cal/serving   193   *Serves 6-7*

Serve it for a party and no one will miss the normal baked dish with white sauce.

600 gms chicken with bones (will give approx. 300 gms boneless chicken)
1 onion - chopped fine
4 medium tomatoes - ground to a puree
½ cup ready made tomato puree
1 tsp salt
1 tsp red chilli powder

SPINACH LAYER
1 tsp oil
6 cups finely chopped spinach (paalak) - washed and strained well to remove all
water (press spinach in the strainer to drain well)
1 tsp garlic paste or finely chopped
3/4 tsp salt, 3/4 tsp pepper, or to taste

TOPPING
some dry bread crumbs
1 tomato - cut into thin wedges

1. Boil or steam chicken. Cool and shred into small pieces.
2. Chop and puree tomatoes in a mixer.
3. In a pan, add chopped onion, pureed tomatoes, tomato puree, 1 tsp salt and red chilli powder. Give 2-3 boils.
4. Add shredded chicken. Mix well. Give a few boils and cook till nearly dry.
5. Heat 1 tsp oil in a nonstick pan. Add garlic and fry for 1-2 minutes.
6. Add spinach, ¾ tsp salt and ¾ tsp pepper.
7. Cook on high heat till spinach is reduced and all the water has evaporated. The spinach should be dry.
8. Take a baking dish. Spread spinach at the bottom.
9. Spread the prepared chicken on top of the spinach to form a layer.
10. Sprinkle bread crumbs on top of the chicken to cover.
11. Decorate with sliced tomato wedges and bake in a preheated oven at 150°C for 20 minutes.

Note: Instead of chicken, fish can also be used.

Tandoori Platter

Picture on facing page　　　　　Serves 8　　　　　*cal/serving*　113

The platter looks equally appetizing without the wooden skewers too!

250 gm paneer - cut into large (1½") cubes, 2 capsicums - cut into large cubes
8 cherry tomatoes or 1 large tomato - cut into 8 pieces & pulp removed
200 gm (10-12) mushrooms - trim ends of the stalks, leaving them whole
100 gm baby corns - blanched with a pinch of haldi and 1 tsp salt in 3 cups water
1 onion - cut into fours & separated, 1 tbsp oil

MARINADE
1 cup thick curd - hung for 30 minutes
1 tbsp cornflour, 1 tbsp thick ginger-garlic paste
½ tsp black salt, ¼ tsp haldi or tandoori colour
2 tsp tandoori masala, ½ tsp red chilli powder, ¾ tsp salt or to taste

BARBECUE SAUCE
1 tbsp oil or butter, 4-5 flakes garlic - crushed
2 large tomatoes - pureed till smooth, ¼ cup ready made tomato puree
¼ tsp red chilli powder, ½ tsp pepper, ¾ tsp salt or to taste, ¼ tsp sugar
½ tsp worcestershire sauce, ½ tsp soya sauce

1. Rub oil generously on a wire rack or grill of the oven.
2. Mix all ingredients of the marinade. Add paneer, mushrooms and babycorns to the marinade and mix well to coat the marinade. Remove from the bowl and arrange on the rack or on all greased wooden skewers. In the remaining marinade which is sticking to the sides of the bowl, add onion, capsicum and tomatoes. Leave these in the bowl itself. Marinate all for atleast ½ hour.
3. Grill paneer and vegetables in the oven at 210°C/410°F for 12-15 minutes or roast in a gas tandoor, spooning a little oil (basting) on them in between.
4. For the barbecue sauce, heat oil or butter in a kadhai. Add garlic and stir. Add tomatoes, tomato puree and red chilli powder and cook for 5 minutes till well blended. Add all other ingredients and ½ cup water to get a thin sauce. Boil. Simmer for 2 minutes. Remove from fire and keep aside.
5. At serving time, heat 1 tbsp oil in a non stick wok or a large nonstick kadhai and add the onion and capsicum. Toss for 1-2 minutes. Reduce flame. Add grilled paneer, mushroom and babycorns. Keep them spread out in the wok on fire for 3-4 minutes on low heat, stirring occasionally. Add the tomatoes.
6. To serve, put some hot sauce on the serving plate. Arrange grilled vegetables on the sauce directly or on skewers again. Pour some hot sauce over the vegetables. Serve at once. You may serve the vegetables on rice too.

Tandoori Fish

Serves 4-6   cal/serving   103

A delicious and a popular fish preparation.

½ kg fish - cut into 2" x 1" pieces

1st MARINADE
juice of 1 lemon
½ tsp salt & ½ tsp chilli powder to taste

2nd MARINADE
½ cup curd - hung for 30 minutes and squeezed
2 tbsp ginger-garlic paste
1 tbsp dry besan (gram flour)
½ tsp ajwain (carom seeds)
3/4 tsp salt, ½ tsp chilli powder
few drops of orange red colour

1. Wash the fish with 1 tbsp besan and some lemon juice to remove the fishy odour. Remove on a kitchen towel and pat dry.
2. Ist Marinade : Place the fish in a vessel, add lemon juice, salt and chilli powder. Keep aside for ½ hour.
3. 2nd Marinade : Later add garlic-ginger paste, hung curd, besan, ajwain, salt, chilli powder and colour. Rub well.
4. Keep aside for 3-4 hours in the refrigerator.
5. Heat a gas tandoor on gas or an electric oven to 200°C.
6. Place them on a greased wire rack and roast till coating turns dry and golden brown, for about 10-15 minutes. Baste with a little oil in between.
7. Sprinkle with tandoori masala or chaat masala or crushed kasoori methi. Serve hot with hari chutney.

Broccoli Tikka

cal/serving 20   *Serves 12*

500 gm (2 medium heads) broccoli- cut into medium florets with long stalks
1 tomato - cut into wedges, to garnish

1ST MARINADE
juice of 1 lemon (1 tbsp)
3/4 tsp ajwain (carom seeds)
1 tsp salt and ½ tsp red chilli powder

2ND MARINADE
1 cup thick curd - hung for 15 minutes or more and squeezed to remove all water
1 tbsp cornflour
1 tbsp ginger-garlic paste
½ tsp red chilli powder
3/4 tsp salt
1 tsp tandoori masala

1. Boil 5-6 cups of water in a large pan. Add 2 tsp salt and 1 tsp sugar to the water. Add broccoli pieces to the boiling water. As soon as the boil returns, remove from fire. Drain. Wipe the pieces well with a clean kitchen towel or on a paper napkin till well dried.
2. Spread the broccoli on a tray and sprinkle the ingredients of the 1st marinade. Marinate the broccoli for 15 minutes.
3. Drain the broccoli of any excess juice.
4. Mix all the ingredients of the 2nd marinade in a large pan. Add the broccoli to it and mix well. Keep in the refrigerator till the time of serving.
5. Before serving, rub the grill of the oven or tandoor with some oil. Heat a gas oven and grill for 10 minutes or grill in a preheated electric oven at 210°C/410°F only for 10 minutes. Do not over grill it, it turns too dry. Serve hot garnished with tomato wedges.

Grilled Sesame Chicken

Serves 8   *cal/serving*   157

The toasted sesame seeds lend a toasted nutty flavour to the chicken.

1 chicken (700-800 gm) - cut into 8 pieces
3 tbsp til (sesame seeds)
3 tbsp ginger-garlic paste
½ cup thick curd
1 tbsp oil
1 tbsp finely chopped coriander leaves
½ tsp black salt
salt to taste
½ tsp chaat masala

1. Roast the sesame seeds on a hot tawa or a pan till light brown, stirring constantly. Remove from tawa and keep aside.
2. Wash and pat dry the chicken pieces on a paper napkin. Make small cuts at 3-4 places.
3. Whip curd till smooth. Add ginger-garlic paste, chopped coriander, chaat masala, black salt, salt, toasted sesame seeds and oil to the curd.
4. Marinate the chicken pieces with this mixture for 2-3 hours in the fridge.
5. Heat the gas tandoor and grill the chicken by placing on a the wire rack for 20 minutes or till tender.

OR

Heat the oven at 180°C. Grease the wire rack of the oven and place the pieces on the wire rack. Place a drip tray underneath for the drippings. Place wire rack in the centre of the oven and heat the elements on the top and bottom. Grill till chicken turns tender.
6. Garnish with onion rings, chopped mint and lemon wedges.

Paneer Tikka

cal/serving   116   Serves 6

300 gm paneer - cut into 1½" squares and 3/4" thick pieces
1 small capsicum - cut into 1" pieces
2 onions - each cut into 8 pieces and then separated
½ cup curd (yogurt) - hung for 30 minutes in a thin cloth
1 tbsp oil
½ tsp jeera powder (ground cumin seeds)
1 tsp lemon juice
½ tsp salt, or to taste
½ tsp kala namak, 1 tbsp tandoori masala
a few drops of orange colour or a pinch of haldi

GRIND TOGETHER
1" piece ginger
5-6 flakes garlic
1-2 dried, whole red chillies - soaked for 10 minutes

1. Drain the soaked red chillies. Grind ginger, garlic and red chillies to a paste.
2. Transfer the paste to a mixing bowl. To the paste, add hung dahi, oil, jeera powder, lemon juice, salt, kala namak, tandoori masala and colour or haldi.
3. Marinate paneer, capsicum and onion pieces in it for at least 2 hours.
4. At the time of serving, grill paneer pieces by placing them on a grill rack brushed with some oil or arrange on oiled skewers. After 5-7 minutes, baste paneer with some oil and change sides. Now put the vegetables also in the oven with the paneer.
5. Grill the paneer till it starts getting crisp from the sides. Remove the vegetables and the paneer from the oven.
6. Arrange hot paneer and vegetables in a serving platter and sprinkle some chaat masala. Serve hot.

Peas, Broccoli & Mushroom Au Gratin

Serves 4   *cal/serving*   120

200 gm mushrooms - sliced
250 gms broccoli (1 small flower) - broken into small florets with a little stalk
3/4 cup shelled peas
1 tomato - cut into round slices
1 tsp oregano or red chilli flakes
1 tsp butter

SAUCE
1 tbsp cornflour
1½ tbsp maida
1½ tbsp oil or melted butter
2½ cups milk
2 tbsp chopped coriander
½ onion - very finely chopped
½ tsp peppercorns - crushed roughly
3/4 tsp salt, or to taste
1 tsp tomato ketchup

1. Boil 4-5 cups water with 2 tsp salt. Add peas and boil till almost done. Add the broccoli florets and give just one boil. Remove from fire and strain. Let them be in the strainer to drain out the water nicely.

2. Heat 1 tsp butter in a non stick pan or a kadhai. Spread the butter on the base of the pan or kadhai. Add mushrooms and stir fry for 3-4 minutes till light brown. While stir frying the mushrooms, keep them spaced out and do not let them be in a heap, overlapping each other. Add the boiled broccoli pieces also and saute for a minute. Add ¼ tsp salt and ¼ tsp pepper. Remove from fire. Remove the vegetables from the pan or kadhai and keep aside.

3. To prepare the sauce, dissolve cornflour in a little milk and keep aside. Heat butter or oil in the pan. Add maida and stir fry on low heat for a minute. Add milk, stirring continuously. Add the cornflour paste. Add chopped coriander, onion, peppercorns and salt also. Mix well and let it boil. Reduce heat, stir continuously, for 5 minutes till the sauce turns a little thick and coats the spoon.

4. Add the boiled peas and tomato ketchup. Cook for 2-3 minutes on low flame.

5. Arrange the broccoli and mushrooms at the bottom of a greased baking dish.

6. Pour the peas in sauce over them. Arrange tomato slices overlapping each other.

7. Sprinkle some oregano or crushed peppercorns. Bake in a hot oven at 200°C till golden brown.

Tinda Tandoori

cal/serving 73   *Serves 6*

½ kg medium size tinda
½ tsp haldi, 1½ tsp salt
4 cups water

FILLING
2 tsp oil
½ tsp jeera (cumin seeds)
2" piece cabbage - shredded (½ cup)
½ cup peas - boiled
2 small potatoes - boiled and mashed
½ tsp red chilli powder, ¾ tsp salt, ½ tsp garam masala, ¾ tsp amchoor
1 tsp tandoori masala
1 tsp kishmish (raisins) - optional
1 green chilli - deseeded and chopped

1. Peel the tindas. Scoop them.
2. Add ½ tsp haldi and 1½ tsp salt to 4 cups water. Add tindas to the boiling water and cook till just done. Do not overcook.
3. To prepare the filling, heat 2 tsp oil. Add ½ tsp jeera, let it turn golden. Add a pinch of haldi. Mix and add shredded cabbage. Stir fry for a while and remove from fire.
4. To the cabbage, add boiled peas, boiled-mashed potatoes, red chillies, salt, garam masala and amchoor.
5. Add tandoori masala, raisins and green chillies. Mix well.
6. Brush the outside of the tindas with a little oil.
7. Fill the stuffing in tindas, heaping it a little.
8. Bake for 15-20 minutes in a moderate oven at 200°C and serve hot.

Vegetables on a bed of Spinach

Picture on page 109   *Serves 4*   *cal/serving*   113

SPINACH LAYER
350 gm (½ bundle) paalak (spinach)
½ tbsp oil or butter
1 tsp garlic (6-7 flakes) - crushed & chopped, 1-2 green chillies - chopped
salt & pepper to taste

OTHER VEGETABLES
2 cups finely chopped mixed vegetables (½ carrot, ¼ of a cauliflower,
¼ cup shelled peas, 5-6 beans)
1 tej patta (bay leaf), 1" stick dalchini (cinnamon)
2 cups milk

SAUCE
1½ tbsp cornflour and 1 tbsp maida dissolved in ½ cup milk
1 tbsp mozzarella or pizza cheese - grated
1 tbsp butter
1 tsp salt, ½ tsp pepper and ½ tsp mustard, or to taste
¼ cup dried bread crumbs

1. Heat oven to 200°C. Discard the stems of spinach and wash leaves well under running water. Finely chop the spinach leaves. Pat dry the leaves.
2. Heat oil or butter. Add garlic and green chillies. Stir and add the spinach. Cook till water evaporates. Sprinkle some salt & pepper. Remove from heat.
3. In a small oven proof dish, spread the cooked spinach.
4. Heat 2 cups of milk in a heavy bottomed sauce pan with a bay leaf and cinnamon stick. Bring the milk to a boil and add the chopped vegetables. Reduce heat and simmer covered till vegetables are done.
5. Meanwhile dissolve cornflour and maida in the remaining ½ cup of milk.
6. When vegetables get just cooked (do not make them too soft), add the dissolved cornflour and maida to the vegetables. Cook till sauce thickens.
7. Add grated cheese, butter, salt, pepper and mustard. Remove from heat. Discard the bay leaf and cinnamon stick.
8. Pour the cooked vegetables on the spinach and level with a spoon.
9. Sprinkle bread crumbs. Bake for 8 minutes at 210°C. Serve with a bread basket.

SNACKS & STARTERS

Mushroom Balls

Serves 6   *cal*/*serving*   21

A light appetizer. Choose slightly big sized mushrooms so that they can be stuffed easily.

12 (200 gm) fresh mushrooms of a slightly bigger size

FILLING
4 tbsp grated cheese (20 gm)
5-6 peppercorns - crushed coarsely
1 tbsp very finely chopped coriander or parsley
2 pinches of salt

COATING
1 egg white - beaten well with a pinch of salt (see note below)
4 tbsp dry bread crumbs
1 tbsp finely chopped coriander or parsley
1 tsp (til) sesame seeds
a pinch of haldi, ¼ tsp salt

1. Wash mushrooms well. To remove the stem, first push the stem to the right and then to the left and then pull it up. The stem will come out leaving a hollow in the cap.
2. Discard stems. Make a deeper and wider hollow in the mushroom cap with the back of a spoon. Keep mushrooms aside on a paper napkin to absorb any water present.
3. Mix all the ingredients of the filling and keep aside.
4. Stuff each mushroom with the filling. Press gently.
5. Mix bread crumbs with coriander, til seeds, haldi and salt. Keep aside.
6. Dip the stuffed mushroom in beaten egg white or maida batter.
7.   Roll in bread crumb mixture, covering the filling as well as the sides.
8.   Bake in a hot oven at 220⁰C for 9-10 minutes in a greased oven proof glass dish or on a greased wire rack till golden.
9. To serve, insert a tooth pick from the side.
10. Serve hot on a bed of shredded lettuce or cabbage.

Note: If you want to avoid the egg white coating, mix 1 tbsp maida in 3-4 tbsp water to make a thin coating batter. Add a little salt and red chilli powder to the batter.

Anaarkali Aloo: Recipe on page 24 ➢

Low Cal Chicken Club Sandwiches

Serves 4   *cal/serving*   77

The mayonnaise has been replaced with low fat curd.

1 chicken breast - boiled and flaked
3/4 cup thick curd - hung for 30 minutes and whipped till smooth
½ onion - chopped very finely
1 tsp mustard paste, 1 tsp chilli-garlic tomato sauce
salt and pepper to taste
6 bread slices, preferably brown - toasted or put under a grill till brown
4 lettuce leaves
a few cucumber and tomato slices
2 hard boiled eggs - cut into slices

1. To boil the chicken, place the chicken breast with ¼ cup water and a little salt in a pressure cooker and give 2 whistles. Remove from heat. Cool and shred chicken into very small pieces.

2. Keep the shredded chicken and the chopped onion in a bowl and add enough whipped curd to get a paste, thick enough for the filling.

3. Adjust seasonings of the filling by adding a dash of pepper, salt, mustard and chilli tomato sauce. Keep the seasonings of the filling a little strong because it may taste bland when applied on the bread.

4. Spread some mixture on a toasted bread slice. Keep a lettuce leaf on top. Arrange some tomato slices on top and sprinkle some salt and pepper on them.

5. Cover with another slice. Place egg slices and sprinkle some salt & pepper on them. Place another lettuce leaf and then arrange kheera slices on the leaf.

6. Place another toast on it. Press well. Cut into 4 small triangles. Secure each sandwich with a toothpick.

7. Repeat with the other 3 slices to make another sandwich. Cut it also in the same way. Serve.

Instant Dhokla

cal/serving 116   *Serves 8*

Yellow dhokla prepared instantly from besan, eno fruit salt and soda bi-carb.

1½ cups besan (gram flour)
½ tsp haldi (turmeric powder)
1 tsp salt, 1 tsp sugar
2 tsp chilli-ginger paste (1" piece ginger & 2 green chillies ground together)
3/4 cup water
¼ tsp soda-bicarb, 1½ tsp eno fruit salt, 2 tsp lemon juice
1 tbsp oil mixed with 4 tbsp water

TEMPERING
1½ tbsp oil
1 tsp rai (mustard seeds)
2-3 green chillies - slit into 2 long pieces
3/4 cup water, 1 tsp sugar, 2 tsp lemon juice
2-3 tbsp freshly grated coconut, 2-3 tbsp chopped coriander

1. Sift besan through a fine sieve to make it light and free of any lumps.
2. Mix besan, haldi, salt, sugar, chilli-ginger paste and water to a smooth batter.
3. Grease a 7" diameter thali (a small thali) with oil.
4. Heat 1 tbsp oil with 4 tbsp water and add to the batter. Beat well.
5. Add eno fruit salt and soda-bicarb to the above batter and pour lemon juice over it. Beat well for a few seconds.
6. Immediately pour this mixture in the greased thali. Level the batter with a knife. Boil 2-3 cups water in a pan and place the thali of batter over it. Cover the thali and steam for 12-13 minutes on medium heat, till the back of a spoon inserted in the dhokla comes out clean. Remove from fire and leave the dhokla covered for 5 minutes.
7. Cool and cut into 1½" diamond shaped pieces. Carefully remove the pieces and arrange on the serving platter.
8. To temper, heat oil, add rai. As rai splutters, add green chillies. Add water, sugar and lemon juice. Boil. Pour tempering on the dhoklas.
9. Sprinkle chopped coriander and freshly grated coconut. Serve after a while so that the water gets absorbed and the dhokla turns soft.

Stuffed Khandvi

Serves 8   *cal/serving* 94

Easy to make, small stuffed rolls made from gram flour cooked in butter milk.

½ cup besan (gram flour)
½ cup curd (not too sour) mixed with 1 cup water to get 1½ cups butter milk
¼ tsp haldi (turmeric powder), ¼ tsp jeera powder (cumin seeds)
½ tsp dhania powder, a pinch of hing (asafoetida) powder, 1 tsp salt

PASTE
½" piece ginger, 1-2 green chillies

FILLING
1 tbsp oil, ½ tsp rai
2 tbsp grated fresh coconut, 1 tbsp grated carrot
1 tsp kishmish - chopped, 1 tbsp chopped coriander, 2 pinches salt

CHOWNK (TEMPERING)
1½ tbsp oil, ½ tsp rai (mustard seeds), 2-3 green chillies - cut into thin long pieces
a few coriander leaves, 1 tbsp grated fresh coconut

1. Mix besan with 1½ cups buttermilk till smooth. Add haldi, jeera, dhania powder hing and salt. Add the ginger-chilli paste also.
2. Prepare a rectangular tray for setting the khandavi, by spreading a cling film (plastic sheet) on the backside of 1 big tray or 2 small trays.
3. Keep the besan-curd mixture on low heat in a non stick pan. Cook this mixture for about 25 minutes, stirring, till the mixture becomes very thick and translucent. Drop 1 tsp mixture on the tray and spread. Let it cool for a while and check if it comes out easily. If it does, remove the mixture from fire, otherwise cook for another 5 minutes. Remove from fire.
4. While the mixture is still hot, quickly spread the mixture as thinly and evenly as possible on the cling film. Level it with a knife.
5. For the filling, heat oil. Add rai. After it crackles, add coconut, carrot, kishmish and chopped coriander. Add salt. Mix. Remove from fire.
6. After the mixture on the tray cools, cut breadthwise into 2" wide strips. Neaten the outside border lines (edges) of the rectangle by cutting them straight.
7. Put 1 tsp filling at one end of the strip. Roll each strip, loosening with a knife initially, to get small cylinders. Arrange them in the serving platter.
8. Prepare the tempering by heating oil in a small vessel. Add rai. When rai splutters, add green chillies. Remove from fire and pour the oil on the khandavis arranged in the plate. Garnish with coconut & coriander.

Chicken Fingers

cal/serving   109   Serves 5-6

400 gms chicken (preferably breasts - cut into 2-3" long pieces, can use boneless
cut into fingers or can use whole chicken pieces)
2 tsp garlic paste, 1 tsp salt
1½ tsp pepper, 1 tbsp vinegar, ½ cup skim milk
3 tbsp fresh dhania chopped finely
2 cups cornflakes - crushed coarsely

1. Wash chicken. Squeeze gently and pat dry on a kitchen towel to dry out all the water.
2. Add vinegar, garlic paste, salt and pepper to the chicken. Mix well. Let it marinate for 4-5 hours in the fridge.
3. Crush cornflakes coarsely. Mix chopped dhania to it.
4. Dip chicken pieces in milk. Roll in cornflakes so that cornflakes coat the chicken pieces.
5. Lightly grease a baking dish/tray.
6. Place pieces on the tray and bake in a hot oven at 230°C for 20-25 minutes or till chicken is tender.

Methi Chicken Chat

cal/serving   127   Serves 4-5

Delicious aromatic snack which can be served as the main dish also.

500 gms chicken - cut into small pieces
1 tsp oil
½" piece ginger - chopped finely
½ tsp salt (adjust to taste), ½ tsp pepper powder (adjust to taste)
2 tbsp kasoori methi (dried fenugreek leaves)
2 tbsp lemon juice
1 tbsp fresh chopped dhania

1. Heat oil in a nonstick pan. Add finely chopped ginger. Fry for 1-2 minutes.
2. Add chicken and fry for 1-2 minutes. Cover and lower heat. Cook till the chicken is tender.
3. Add all the ingredients except fresh dhania. Increase heat and dry the chicken completely. Serve hot, garnished with fresh chopped coriander.

Fruity Cherry Tomatoes

Serves 15   *cal/serving*   24

Cherry tomatoes are very tiny tomatoes, about the size of a big cherry.

30-40 (½ kg) cherry tomatoes
½ apple - peeled & very finely diced
2 tbsp channa dal, 100 gms paneer (of toned milk) - grated
1 tsp mustard paste
½ tsp salt, 8-10 peppercorns - crushed, a few coriander leaves
a few cocktail sticks or tooth picks

1. To boil channa dal, boil 3/4 cup water with ½ tsp salt. Add dal. Boil. Cover and cook on low heat for about 12-15 minutes or till the dal is just done. Strain and keep the dal aside.
2. Cut a thin slice of the tomato from top. Scoop the pulp. If you wish, rub a pinch of salt inside the hollow tomatoes.
3. Mix dal, paneer and apple. Add mustard paste, salt & pepper to taste.
4. Fill the mixture in tomatoes.
5. Insert a toothpick in each tomato from the side. Serve at room temperature on lettuce or cabbage leaves. In winters you may heat them in the oven or microwave to serve them warm.

Spiced Baby Corns

Serves 6   *cal/serving*   45

200 gm baby corns
1 tbsp green coriander paste made by crushing a few coriander leaves
½ cup dahi (of toned milk)
1½ tsp garlic paste, 2 green chillies - deseeded and chopped finely
1 tsp salt, or to taste, a pinch of haldi, some chaat masala - to sprinkle

1. Pressure cook all ingredients together, except chaat masala, to give 1 whistle. Remove from fire.
2. After the pressure drops, open the cooker and dry the water.
3. Serve sprinkled with some chaat masala.

Note: If baby corns are not available, cut the regular corn into 1½" pieces and pressure cook to give 1 whistle and then keep on low flame for 8-10 minutes. Choose tender corns.

Chicken Canapes

cal/serving   159   *Serves 6*

1 breast of chicken - deboned (boneless) and shredded
1 tsp oil
½ cup thinly sliced onion
1 tsp finely chopped ginger
1 tsp garlic - chopped finely
1 large tomato - blanched, peeled and chopped finely
1-2 green chillies - chopped finely
salt and pepper to taste
1 tsp finely chopped fresh mint leaves
6 slices bread - toasted in the toaster or oven or 12 cream cracker biscuits

1. To boil the chicken, place the chicken breast with ¼ cup water and a little salt in a pressure cooker and give 2 whistles. Remove from heat. Cool and shred chicken into very small pieces.
2. Heat oil in a non stick pan. Add onion, ginger, garlic and cook for 1-2 minutes.
3. When onion is soft, add shredded chicken, salt and pepper to taste, tomato and green chillies. Cook till dry. Remove from fire.
4. Add mint leaves. Mix well.
5. Toast bread in an oven or toaster.
6. Cut into desired shapes, triangular, square or rounds.
7. Spread prepared chicken on the toast, garnish with a sprig of mint and serve with mint chutney.

Note: A quick snack can be made with any left over chicken also. Instead of chicken, shredded & boiled mutton or mushrooms can also be used.

Momos

Makes 12　　　　　　　*cal/serving* 110

DOUGH
1 cup maida (plain flour), 1 tbsp oil, ¼ tsp salt

FILLING
1 onion - finely chopped, 6 mushrooms - chopped very finely
1 tsp ginger garlic paste, 2 green chillies - finely chopped
1 large carrot - very finely chopped or grated
2½ cups very finely chopped cabbage (1 small cabbage)
2 tbsp oil, 1 tsp salt & 1 tsp pepper powder, or to taste

RED HOT CHUTNEY
4-5 dry, Kashmiri red chillies - soaked in ¼ cup warm water
6-8 flakes garlic, 1 tsp saboot dhania (coriander seeds), 1 tsp jeera (cumin seeds)
1 tbsp oil, ½ tsp salt, 1 tsp sugar, 3 tbsp vinegar, ½ tsp soya sauce

1. Sift maida with salt. Add oil and knead with enough water to make a stiff dough of rolling consistency, as that for puris.
2. Heat 2 tbsp oil in the kadhai for the filling. Add the chopped onion. Fry till it turns soft. Add mushrooms and cook further for 2 minutes. Add carrot, green chillies & ginger-garlic paste. Mix well and add the cabbage. Stir fry on high flame for 3 minutes. Add salt, pepper to taste. Remove from fire and keep aside.
3. Make marble sized balls and roll as thin as possible, to make about 5 inch rounds. Put 1 heaped tbsp of the filling. Pick up the sides into loose folds like frills and keep collecting each fold in the centre, to give a flattened ball (like a kachorie).
4. Place the momos in a greased steamer and steam it in a pressure cooker with 2 cups water without the whistle for 3-4 minutes.
5. Remove each momo with a slotted spoon and place in a plate, keeping them spread out in the plate. Dry them under the fan, on both sides.
6. The momos can be had as it is, that is steamed, or it can be baked in the oven at 200°C for 5 minutes till light golden on the edges.
7. Serve with red hot chutney. For the chutney, grind the soaked red chillies along with the water, garlic, dhania, jeera, oil, salt and sugar. Add soya sauce and vinegar to taste.

Chicken Momos

To make chicken momos, saute ½ cup boiled and diced chicken instead of mushrooms. Stir fry for 3-4 minutes till cooked and then proceed further.

Mince Dumplings

cal/serving 60   *Gives 24 Kebabs*

500 gms keema (minced lamb)
1½ tsp ginger-garlic paste
½ tsp dhania powder
1 tsp jeera (cumin seeds) powder
1 tsp salt
2 tbsp chopped fresh dhania
1 tsp red chilli powder
1 tsp salt, or to taste
3-4 green chillies - finely chopped
2 tbsp level besan (gramflour)
1-2 tsp oil

1. Wash keema well. Strain and squeeze out all the water. (It is essential to squeeze out the water well otherwise it will be difficult to make balls).
2. Mix all the ingredients except oil to the keema. Mix well and make small balls.
3. Take a pressure cooker and grease the bottom.
4. Place the balls in the pressure cooker. They can be piled on top of each other.
5. Close cooker and give 1 whistle. Lower heat and let it simmer for 5-7 minutes.
6. When pressure drops, open cooker and remove dumplings gently.
7. Take a non stick pan. Heat 1-2 tsp oil, add balls and gently brown them on all sides.
8. Serve hot with mint chutney.

Note: The dumplings will leave some water when cooked. If you like, after opening the cooker, dry the water or discard it.

Instant Suji Utthapams

Serves 4-5   *cal/serving*   88

Make tiny utthapams because it is difficult to turn them while cooking if they are big in size. You can serve them as cute little pancakes for tea!

BATTER
½ cup thick rawa suji (coarse semolina)
¼ tsp baking powder
¼ - ½ tsp salt or to taste
½ cup curd (approx.)
1 tbsp oil - to sprinkle

TOPPING (MIX TOGETHER)
1 small onion - very finely chopped
½ capsicum - very finely chopped
1 tomato - finely chopped
½ tsp salt, or to taste
1 tsp til (sesame seeds)

1. Mix suji with curd to get a thick batter of a soft dropping consistency.
2. Add baking powder and salt and beat well. Keep aside for 10 minutes.
3. Add 2 tbsp water if the batter is too thick, but keep the batter thick of a soft dropping consistency.
4. Heat a non stick tawa on low flame. Sprinkle a little oil on the tawa. Wipe it clean with a napkin.
5. Keeping the flame low, drop 1 tbsp of batter on the tawa to make a tiny pancake of 1½-2" diameter. It should not be too thin, keep it a little thick like an utthappum.
6. Drop more tbsps of batter on the tawa, keeping space between them. Make about 4 at a time.
7. When bubbles arise on the pancakes and the sides cook a little, sprinkle some topping mixture on all the pancakes. Press gently.
8. Put 2-3 drops of oil on each pancake.
9. Carefully over turn the pancakes to cook the other side. Press gently.
10. Cook on very low heat to cook the pancakes properly.
11. Remove the pancakes on to a plate after 3-4 minutes.
12. Serve hot for breakfast, as an evening snack or as an appetizer.

Dapka Kadhi: Recipe on page 20 ➢

Spiced Button Idlis

Serves 8   *cal/serving*   98

Special saanchas (moulds) which make tiny (button) idlis are available these days. Enjoy these idlis without sambhar or chutney.

1 cup suji (semolina)
1½ cups curd, approx.
3/4 tsp Eno fruit salt
2 tbsp chopped hara dhania (fresh coriander)
3/4 tsp salt

TEMPERING (CHHOWNK)
2 tsp oil
1 tsp rai (small brown mustard seeds)
½ tsp red chilli flakes or chilli powder
7-8 saboot kali mirch (peppercorns) - coarsely crushed
a few curry leaves

1. Mix suji with curd to get a smooth batter of a soft dropping consistency. If the mixture is too thick, then add some more curd.
2. Add Eno fruit salt, hara dhania and salt. Mix well.
3. Immediately spoon the batter into the greased mould and steam for 14-15 minutes on **medium flame** till a knife inserted in it comes out clean. Cool and remove from mould and keep aside.
4. To temper the idlis, heat oil in a clean non stick kadhai or pan. Add rai and let it splutter for 1 minute. Remove from fire.
5. Add curry leaves. Add the idlis.
6. Sprinkle red chilli flakes and crushed peppercorns.
7. Return to fire. Mix well for 2-3 minutes. Serve hot.

Paper Fried Chicken

cal/serving 51   *Serves 6*

Although fried, no oil touches the chicken as it is fried in foil packets.

200 gms chicken - cut into small pieces
1 tbsp chopped red capsicum
1 tbsp chopped green capsicum
4-5 flakes garlic - crushed
½ tsp crushed ginger
½ tsp salt, ¼ tsp pepper
1 tbsp soya sauce
1 tbsp sherry (optional)
¼ tsp ajinomoto (optional)
1 tbsp cornflour
1 egg
aluminium foil

1. Mix all ingredients along with the chicken and let it marinate for 1-2 hours.
2. Cut aluminium foil into square pieces of 6" x 6".
3. Divide filling into 6-8 portions.
4. Place one portion of the filling in the centre of a piece of foil. Fold like an envelope.
5. Deep fry in medium hot oil, keeping the packet in oil for 3-4 minutes so that the chicken gets cooked. Remove from oil.
6. Arrange on a bed of lettuce or garnish with capsicum strips.
7. The envelops can be served closed or partially opened.

Note :   Instead of chicken, prawns, fish, mushrooms or paneer can be used.

Grilled Curd Cheese Fingers

Serves 4-5   *cal/serving 70*

**1 cup thick curd (prepared from toned milk) - hung for 1-2 hours
3-4 tbsp cabbage - shredded, 2-3 tbsp carrot - grated
1 green chilli - deseeded and finely chopped
salt and pepper to taste
2 tbsp green mint or coriander chutney
6 slices bread, preferably brown bread**

1. Beat hung curd in a bowl till smooth.
2. Add cabbage, carrot, green chilli, salt & pepper. Mix well. Add a little extra salt, otherwise the fingers taste bland.
3. Spread the curd mix generously on a slice.
4. Spread some chutney on another slice. Place the chutney slice, with the chutney side down on the curd slice. Press well.
5. Grill in a sandwich toaster or in the oven on the wire rack till browned.
6. Cut into 4 fingers and serve hot. Repeat with the other 4 slices.

Sesame Potato Fingers

Serves 6   *cal/serving 59*

An appetizer which is easy to cook and delicious to eat!

**4 slices of brown bread
1 tsp kale til (black sesame seeds) or white sesame seeds**

**MIX TOGETHER
2 boiled potatoes - grated, 1 tsp tomato sauce
1 green chilli - deseeded and finely chopped
2 tbsp chopped hara dhania (fresh coriander)
½ onion - very finely chopped, ½ tomato - very finely chopped
3/4 tsp salt, ¼ tsp pepper and ½ tsp chaat masala, or to taste**

1. Press some potato mixture on the bread.
2. Sprinkle some sesame seeds. Grill in an oven till the toast turns crisp.
3. Cut each slice into 3 long fingers and serve hot.

Note: For children, you may put a slice of cheese on the potatoes and sprinkle with sesame seeds. Grill and serve.

Mango Submarine Special

Picture on page 1　　　　　*Serves 4-5*　　　　　*cal/serving 145*

1 long garlic bread - cut lengthwise to get 2 thin, long pieces
1½ tbsp mango chutney (fun food)
1 kheera - cut into round slices without peeling
2 firm tomatoes - cut into round slices
150 gm paneer - cut into ¼" round slices with a kulfi mould cover
few poodina (mint) leaves to garnish - dipped in chilled water
½ tbsp butter - softened

SPRINKLE ON PANEER
¼ tsp haldi
½ tsp chilli powder
½ tsp salt
1 tsp chaat masala powder

1. Spread butter lightly on the cut surface of both the pieces of garlic bread, as well as a little on the sides.
2. Place the garlic breads in the oven at 200°C on a wire rack for 10-12 minutes till crisp and light brown on the cut surface. Keep aside.
3. Cut paneer into ¼" thick slices and then cut the slices into round pieces with a kulfi mould (saancha) cover or a biscuit cutter.
4. Sprinkle the paneer on both sides with some chilli powder, salt, haldi and chaat masala.
5. At serving time - saute paneer pieces on a non stick pan without oil, till golden brown from the sides. Keep stirring, do not burn the paneer pieces while sauting (You can use minimum amount of oil to fry the paneer pieces, this is optional)
6. To assemble the submarine, apply 1 tbsp mango chutney on each garlic bread.
7. Sprinkle some chaat masala on the kheera and tomato pieces. Sprinkle some chat masala on the paneer also.
8. Place a piece of paneer, then kheera, then tomato and keep repeating all three in the same sequence so as to cover the loaf. Keep paneer, kheera and tomato, slightly overlapping. Insert fresh mint leaves in between the vegetables, so that they show. Serve.

Note:　　Mango chutney is available in bottles in stores.

Vegetable Gold Coins

Serves 6   *cal/serving   60*

6 bread slices
1 large potato - boiled and grated
1 small onion - chopped finely
1 carrot - grated
1 capsicum - chopped very finely (diced)
2 tsp soya sauce
2 tsp tomato sauce
½ tsp pepper
¼ tsp chilli powder
3/4 tsp salt, or to taste
2 tsp sesame seeds (til) - to sprinkle

1. In a non stick pan add onions with ¼ cup water. Cook till onions turn soft and the water dries.
2. Add vegetables. Cook for 2 minutes on low flame.
3. Reduce heat. Add potatoes, soya sauce, tomato sauce, salt, pepper and chilli powder. Cook for 2-3 minutes. Keep aside.
4. With a biscuit cutter or a sharp lid, cut out small rounds (about 1½" diameter) of the bread.
5. Spread some potato mixture in a slight heap on the round piece of bread, leaving the edges. Press.
6. Sprinkle sesame seeds. Press.
7. Grill at 180°C for 8 minutes or till bread turns crisp from the underside. Serve, dotted with chilli-garlic or masala chilli tomato sauce.

Honeyed Barbecued Chicken, Fish or Prawns

cal/serving 99   *Serves 4-5*

500 gms prawns (leave whole) or 500 gm chicken or fish - cut into small pieces
1 tbsp honey, salt to taste, 1 tsp pepper powder
2 tsp soya sauce, 1 tsp ginger crushed roughly, 1 tsp garlic crushed roughly
3-4 green chillies - crushed roughly
a little lemon rind - grated (optional)

1. Mix all ingredients and marinate prawns, fish or chicken for 1-2 hours.
2. Barbecue in a hot oven or grill on a greased tray for 10-12 minutes or till cooked.
3. Serve hot on tooth picks.

Barbecued Chicken Drumsticks

cal/serving 143   *Serves 8*

8-10 chicken drumsticks (legs)
2 tbsp oil or butter - to baste

MARINADE
1 onion - grated
salt and chilli flakes or chilli powder, to taste
2 tbsp vinegar, 8 tbsp tomato puree, 3-4 tbsp tomato ketchup
2 tsp worcestershire sauce, 1 tsp oregano

1. Wash and pat dry the chicken on a kitchen towel or a paper napkin.
2. Mix grated onion with all the other ingredients given under marinade. Marinate the chicken pieces in this marinade for 3-4 hours in the refrigerator.
3. Heat oven at 180°C- 200°C or heat a gas tandoor. Place chicken on a baking tray and roast for 20 minutes.
4. Add some oil or melted butter to the left over marinade and baste chicken pieces with this marinade. Grill again for 10 minutes. If using a gas tandoor, place the chicken pieces on the wire rack of the gas tandoor.
5. Cook till the chicken is tender. Serve with onion rings, garnished with parsley or mint.

Note : If you desire to microwave the chicken, microwave on full power for 10 minutes. Baste, turn the pieces & microwave for another 5 minutes more.

Oil free Baby Corn Canapes

Serves 10-12   *cal/serving   60*

1 French Loaf or garlic bread - cut into ¼" thick diagonal slices
50 gm paneer (2" cube) - grated
2 tbsp chopped mint

BABY CORN TOPPING
150 gm baby corns - cut into ¼" thick round slices (1½ cups)
2 tsp vinegar, 2 tsp soya sauce, 1 tsp red chilli sauce
2 tbsp cornflour dissolved in ½ cup water
½ tsp salt, ½ tsp pepper

TOMATO PASTE
6-8 flakes garlic - crushed
¼ tsp red chilli powder
½ cup ready made tomato puree
2 tbsp tomato sauce
1 tsp oregano (dried) or ½ tsp ajwain
½ tsp salt and ½ tsp pepper to taste

1. To prepare the tomato paste, mix all the ingredients and cook on low flame for about 5 minutes, till thick. Keep aside.
2. To prepare the baby corn topping, mix all ingredients, except the baby corns in a heavy bottomed pan or kadhai and then add the sliced baby corns. Keep on fire and cook on low flame, stirring continuously till the sauce coats the baby corns and they get cooked a little.
3. Spread some tomato paste on the slices. Arrange some baby corns in sauce over it. Press.
4. Grate some paneer finely over it. Sprinkle some mint, crushed peppercorns and some salt on the paneer.
5. To serve, grill at 200°C for 7-8 minutes till a little crisp. Do not over grill otherwise they turn too hard. Cut into 2 pieces and serve.

Note: If baby corns are not available, cooked or tinned corn kernels may be substituted.

Unfried Chilly Potatoes

cal/serving 46   *Serves 4-6*

12-15 baby potatoes or 3 small potatoes - boiled & cut into 4 pieces
1 large capsicum - cut into ½" - 3/4" pieces
3-4 flakes garlic - crushed
1 green chilli - deseeded & chopped
¼ tsp red chilli powder
1 tbsp vinegar
2 tsp soya sauce
2 tbsp tomato ketchup
1 tsp red chilli sauce
2-3 tbsp very finely chopped coriander
1 tbsp oil

1. Heat 1 tbsp oil in a wok or a non stick pan. Reduce flame.
2. Add garlic & green chillies. Stir.
3. Shut off the fire. Add red chilli powder, vinegar, soya sauce, tomato ketchup and red chilli sauce.
4. Return to fire. Add ¼ tsp salt and add potatoes. Toss well to mix.
5. Add finely chopped coriander.
6. Cook on medium flame for 3-4 minutes, adding 2 tbsp of water so that the sauces do not burn, till potatoes get coated with the sauce.
7. Reduce flame. Add the capsicum. Mix well. Remove from fire after a minute, otherwise the capsicum changes colour.
8. To serve, add a few tbsp water & heat well. Pass a piece of capsicum, keeping the green side up through a toothpick, then pass a piece of potato, keeping the flat side down. Pass another piece of capsicum to sandwich the potato inbetween the capsicum pieces. Serve hot.

Note : The toothpicks with potato and capsicum can be made in advance and heated at the time of serving in a microwave.

Mutton Balls

Serves 5-6   *cal/serving 147*

½ kg fine keema (lamb mince)
2 tbsp garlic-ginger-green chilli paste
1 tsp garam masala
1 tsp dhania powder (ground coriander)
1 tsp red chilli powder, salt to taste
2 tbsp heaped besan (gram flour)
2 tbsp oil for shallow frying

DRY MASALA COATING
½ tsp chat masala
1 tbsp dhania powder
1 tsp red chilli powder, 1 tsp garam masala

1. Put the mince in a strainer. Pour water to wash and gently press to drain out all the water (if water is not drained out properly, the balls will not bind well and tend to break while pressure cooking).
2. Put the mince in a bowl. Add all the other ingredients except oil. Mix and knead well or put in a mixer blender and blend well.
3. Take a pressure cooker or a pan, oil its bottom well.
4. Take a heaped tbsp of mince in the palm of your hand and bind the mince tightly into balls, squeezing out any excess liquid. Make balls a little bag, as mince tends to shrink after cooking.
5. Arrange them at the bottom of the pressure cooker. Place the balls gently, over lapping one another, if short of space. Do not add water in the cooker, as the mince will leave water.
6. Pressure cook to give 2 whistles and simmer on low flame for 2 minutes. Remove from fire. Let the pressure drop by itself.
7. Gently remove the steamed meat balls. Keep aside.
8. At serving time, add 2 tbsp oil in a non stick pan and stir fry the steamed balls in a pan on medium heat.
9. When they turn brown, sprinkle chaat masala, coriander powder, red chilli powder and garam masala. Cook till dry masala coats the balls.
10. Remove on a plate and garnish with green coriander and lemon wedges. Serve with coriander or mint chutney.

Vegetables in Red Curry (Thai): Recipe on page 52 ➢

Grilled Chilli Prawns

Serves 5-6   *cal/serving* 58

10-12 medium size prawns
3-4 flakes garlic - crushed & chopped finely
½ tsp red chilli flakes
½ tsp salt
½ tsp sugar
2 tbsp lemon juice
1 tbsp chopped coriander
1 tbsp oil
salt to taste

1. Devein and wash the prawns. Pat dry on a paper napkin.
2. Mix all the ingredients in a bowl. Add the prawns and mix them well. Cover and leave to marinate the prawns in it for 1 hour.
3. Arrange the marinated prawns on a baking tray. Bake in a hot oven at 200°C for 10-12 minutes, basting with oil in between.
4. Serve atonce, garnished with lemon wedges and fresh coriander.

Note : Be particular about the baking time, do not over bake.

SOUPS & SALADS

Tomato & Coriander Shorba

Serves 4   *cal/serving*   *100*

A thin tomato soup with the authentic Indian flavour. Coriander adds it's refreshing taste.

1 kg (12 medium) red tomatoes - chopped roughly
400 ml (2½ teacups) water
4 tsp besan (gram flour)
½ cup finely chopped fresh coriander
1 tbsp oil
1 tsp jeera (cumin seeds)
8-10 curry leaves
2-3 green chillies - slit lengthwise
1 tsp sugar or to taste
1 tsp salt or to taste
1 tsp lemon juice or to taste

1. Pressure cook the tomatoes with water to give one whistle. Keep on low flame for 5-7 minutes. Remove from fire.
2. When it cools down, blend in a mixer. Strain and keep tomato juice aside.
3. Add besan to 4 cups water and blend well in the mixer. Keep aside.
4. Heat oil in a pan and reduce flame. Add jeera. Let it turn golden.
5. Add curry leaves, green chillies, tomato juice, water mixed with besan and sugar. Boil.
6. Add coriander leaves & salt to taste.
7. Cook for 4-5 minutes. Add lemon juice to taste. Serve hot.

Kali Mirch Jeera Rasam

cal/serving   24   *Serves 4*

A hot, spicy rasam, delicious as an appetizer.

4 large tomatoes - chopped roughly
3 cups water
2 tsp oil
1 tsp sarson (mustard seeds)
a few curry leaves
8-10 flakes of garlic - chopped & crushed
1 tsp jeera (cumin seeds) - powdered roughly
1 tsp saboot kali mirch (peppercorns) - powdered roughly
¼ tsp haldi (turmeric powder)
1¼ tsp salt, or to taste

1. Boil the tomatoes with 1 cup water in a pan. Simmer for 10 minutes on low flame till tomatoes turn very soft.
2. Remove from fire and mash lightly. Add the remaining 2 cups water & mash a little. Strain the juice through a big strainer into another clean pan. Discard the peels.
3. Powder the jeera & kali mirch coarsely on a chakla belan. Keep aside.
4. Heat 2 tsp oil in a heavy bottomed pan. Add mustard seeds.
5. When it splutters, reduce flame. Add curry leaves and garlic. Fry a little, till garlic changes colour.
6. Add the coarsely powdered jeera and saboot kali mirch. Fry for ½ minute.
7. Add tomato juice to it. Add haldi powder & salt. Boil. Simmer on low flame for 7-8 minutes.
8. Serve hot by adding 1 tsp desi ghee, if desired.

Broccoli & Bean Salad in Mustard Dressing

Serves 4   *cal/serving* 33

VEGETABLES
100 gm (20-25) tender french beans
1 small (250 gm) broccoli
1 tomato or 3-4 strawberries

MUSTARD DRESSING
2 tsp mustard paste
½ tsp peppercorns - crushed
½ tsp salt
juice of 1 large lemon (2½-3 tbsp)
10-15 flakes garlic - sliced finely

1. Mix all ingredients of the dressing together in a small bowl.
2. Thread beans and cut into 1½" long pieces. Cut broccoli into medium florets with a little stalk. Cut strawberries or tomato lengthwise into slices. Remove pulp from tomatoes.
3. Boil 4-5 cups water with 2 tsp salt and 2 tsp sugar.
4. Add beans to the boiling water. As soon as the boil returns, keep the beans boiling for 1 minute.
5. Add broccoli. Remove from fire. Leave vegetables in hot water for 2 minutes.
6. Strain the vegetables. Refresh by taking them out of cold water. Leave in the strainer to drain out all the water.
7. Pat dry the vegetables on a paper napkin and transfer them to a mixing bowl.
8. Add the sliced tomatoes or strawberries.
9. Add the dressing to the vegetables. Toss to mix well. Serve cold.

Creamy Chicken Salad

cal/serving 66   Serves 6

Use hung curd instead of mayonnaise and get a delicious low calorie salad.

2½ cups low fat curd - (hang in a muslin cloth for ½ hour)
2 chicken breast (300 gm)
1 tsp Kashmiri red chilli paste or red chilli powder, 1 tsp mustard paste, or to taste
1 tbsp finely chopped celery or capsicum
1 cup fruit (oranges or chopped pineapple or chopped apple)
1 tsp salt, ½ tsp black pepper powder, or to taste, a little milk

GARNISHING
a few salad/lettuce leaves - chopped

1. Steam/boil chicken and shred it (cut into small pieces) and cool it.
2. Soak 1-2 whole red chillies in water for 1 hour and make a paste of them, alternately you can use red chilli powder.
3. Mix hung curd, salt, pepper, red chilli, mustard paste, chicken, celery and fruit.
4. Use a little milk if the salad seems too thick. Mix well.
5. To serve, place salad in the centre of a plate, surround with shredded lettuce leaves and serve chilled.

Note: If using tinned pineapple, squeeze out all the juice.

Green Papaya Salad

cal/serving 88   Serves 4-6

A classic sweet and hot Thai salad of raw papaya, tomatoes and green beans in a thin tamarind chilli dressing.

3 cups grated hard, raw papaya
1 tomato - cut into 8 pieces and deseeded
½ cup tender green beans (french beans or lobia or chawli) - sliced very finely
¼ cup roasted peanuts - crushed coarsely

TAMARIND CHILLI DRESSING
1 tbsp tamarind pulp, 1 tsp chilli powder, 1 tbsp soya sauce, 2 tbsp lemon juice
2 tbsp sugar, ½ tsp salt, or to taste, 2 tbsp chopped coriander
3-4 green chillies and 1 flake garlic - pounded together

1. Mix all ingredients of the dressing together.
2. Put papaya and all other ingredients in a bowl. Add the dressing and mix well.
3. Cover with a cling film and chill for at least one hour, so that the flavours penetrate.

Chicken Hot & Sour Soup

Serves 4   *cal/serving*   70

You may also make it without shredded chicken, when you do not have chicken at home. Simply increase the shredded cabbage to ½ cup.

4-5 cups chicken stock or water mixed with a chicken seasoning cube
¼ cup boiled and shredded chicken
2 flakes garlic - crushed
¼ cup shredded cabbage
1 small carrot - grated
1 spring onion - chopped finely
3 tbsp cornflour
1 tbsp soya sauce, 1 tbsp vinegar
½ tsp red chilli paste or powder
½ tsp pepper, ½ tsp salt, or to taste
½ tsp ajinomoto (optional)
2 tbsp oil

1. To boil the chicken, place the chicken with a 4-5 cups water and a little salt in a pressure cooker and give 2 whistles. Remove from heat. Cool and shred chicken into very small pieces.

2. Heat 2 tbsp oil in a pan. Add the cabbage, carrot, spring onion & shredded chicken. Saute for ½ minute.

3. Add the chicken stock or water mixed with a chicken seasoning cube.

4. Add soya sauce, vinegar, chilli paste, pepper and ajinomoto to the stock. Stir and give it a boil. Add salt after tasting if a seasoning cube has been added as the cube has a lot of salt in it.

5. Mix cornflour with ½ cup cold water and add to the soup. Boil.

6. Cook on low flame for 4-5 minutes till the soup thickens and the raw smell of cornflour disappears. Serve hot.

Potato Salad

cal/serving 59   *Serves 4*

Potatoes unless fried are not fattening at all! They are rich in carbohydrates which keep you full for a long time, and thus keep you away from snacking in between meals.

250 gms baby potatoes - boiled and peeled
½ cup thick curd - whipped till smooth
½ tsp salt, ½ tsp peppercorns - crushed
2 tbsp mint leaves - finely chopped
½ tsp mustard paste, ½ tsp soya sauce, 3/4 tsp chilli sauce

1. Boil the baby potatoes. Peel them.
2. In a bowl beat the curd well till smooth.
3. To the curd add all other ingredients, except the boiled potatoes. Mix well.
4. Add the boiled potatoes. Mix gently and transfer to a serving dish. Garnish with fresh mint. Serve.

Fruity Salad in Orange Dressing

cal/serving 42   *Serves 4*

½ cup cabbage - chopped, ½ cup carrot - chopped
¼ cup onion - chopped, ½ cup tomatoes - chopped
½ cup grapes or strawberries - halved or chopped
½ cup orange segments

ORANGE DRESSING
1 tbsp oil
¼ cup orange juice (fresh or ready made)
1 tsp lemon juice
2-3 flakes garlic - crushed
½ tsp oregano
½ tsp salt and ½ tsp pepper, or to taste

1. Mix all fruits and vegetables in a large bowl. Chill.
2. Mix all ingredients of the orange dressing in a bottle. Close cap and shake well to mix. Keep aside.
3. An hour before serving, pour the dressing over the fruit and vegetable mixture in the bowl. Toss lightly with two forks. Add more salt and pepper if desired.
4. Refrigerate till serving time.

Clear Chicken & Mushroom Soup

Serves 5   *cal/serving   50*

A tasty soup. Always a hit and so simple to prepare.

200 gms chicken, preferably breast
6 cups water, 1 stalk of lemon grass - chopped, 1" piece ginger - chopped
100 gms mushrooms - cut into paper thin slices
2-3 green chillies - slit long with seeds removed
1 tsp salt, pepper to taste, 3-4 tsp lemon juice (adjust to taste)

1. Place chicken, lemon grass, ginger and water in a cooker and give 4-5 whistles.
2. When pressure drops, strain and separate the chicken from stock.
3. Discard lemon grass and ginger. Pick up the pieces of chicken. Shred chicken very finely as it is a clear soup and the chicken will sink if the pieces are even slightly big.
4. Keep stock on heat. Add sliced mushrooms, shredded chicken, salt, pepper and green chillies. Give 3-4 boils or till mushrooms are just tender. Add lemon juice.
5. Serve hot, garnished with chopped fresh coriander.

Chicken Flower Soup

Serves 4   *cal/serving   68*

Vegetable flowers added to chicken soup make it nourishing as well as appetizing.

150 gms chicken (preferably breast)
½" piece ginger - chopped, 4-5 peppercorns (saboot kali mirch) - crushed
3/4 cup carrot flowers, ½ cup cucumber flowers, 3/4 tsp salt, ¼ tsp pepper
4 tsp lemon juice, 1½ tsp cornflour

1. Place chicken with 4 cups of water, ginger and peppercorns in a cooker and give 3-4 whistles.
2. Strain and separate stock from chicken. Shred the chicken.
3. To make carrot and cucumber flowers, peel and make ridges by removing a little of the vegetable longitudinally at ½" distance. Cut into thin slices horizontally and you will get beautiful flowers. If not, just use carrot and cucumber rounds.
4. Place stock for boiling, add carrots. Cook till just tender.
5. Add shredded chicken, salt, pepper, cornflour dissolved in little water, cucumber flowers. Give 1-2 boils.
6. Add lemon juice. Mix well. Serve hot garnished with parsley.

Vegetables on a bed of Spinach: Recipe on page 76 ➤

Warm Stir Fried Salad

Serves 3-4   *cal/serving* 51

Warm salads are becoming very popular these days. It is fatless, yet delicious & nutritious.

150 gms boneless chicken - cut into ½" strips
3/4 cup cabbage thinly sliced
½ red and ½ yellow capsicum - thinly sliced
1 cup carrot grated
½ tsp salt, ½ tsp pepper (optional)
2-3 tsp lemon juice
some lettuce leaves to serve

MARINADE
1 tsp soya sauce
½ tsp salt, ½ tsp pepper
½" piece ginger - cut into juliennes

1. Marinate chicken strips with ingredients given under marinade for 2-3 hours.
2. Cook chicken along with the marinade together for 2-3 minutes in a non stick pan till chicken is tender.
3. Add vegetables.
4. Add ½ tsp each of salt and pepper.
5. Add 2-3 tsp lemon juice. Cook till just cooked but crunchy.
6. Serve warm garnished with lettuce leaves.

Cottage Cheese Boats

cal/serving   37   *Serves 4*

2 firm, big, longish tomatoes
50 gms paneer - grated (4 tbsp)
1 tbsp chopped coriander
1 tsp finely chopped onion, optional
½ tsp grated ginger (a small piece - grated)
3-4 saboot kali mirch (peppercorns) - crushed
¼ tsp salt, or to taste, a few olives, optional, - to garnish
some parsley or coriander - to garnish

1. Cut the tomatoes into two halves. Scoop out leaving the walls intact. Rub some salt inside and keep them inverted for a few minutes.
2. Gently mix grated paneer with all the other ingredients.
3. Stuff into the tomato shells and press well. Cut into 2 pieces with a sharp knife.
4. Garnish each boat with a slice of olive and a coriander or parsley leaf.

Sprouts in Spicy Honey Dressing

cal/serving   36   *Serves 4*

3 cups (300 gm) moong sprouts or mixed sprouts
2 tsp honey
2 tbsp lemon juice, 2 tsp soya sauce
½-3/4 tsp red chilli powder, 1 tsp salt, or to taste
8-10 saboot kali mirch (peppercorns) - crushed
1 tomato - chopped finely
1 green chilli - chopped finely, 1½" piece ginger - finely grated

GARNISH
greens of 1 spring onion - finely chopped or 1 tbsp chopped coriander

1. Steam the sprouts by placing them on a large stainless steel strainer (colander) on a pan of boiling water for 5-6 minutes till slightly soft. Remove from heat.
2. Transfer sprouts to a bowl. Add all the other ingredients and toss well.
3. Garnish with some finely chopped spring onion greens or coriander.

Note: You can microwave the sprouts instead of steaming them. Wash sprouts. Put in a plastic (polythene) bag. Micro high for 3 minutes.

LOW CALORIE DESSERTS

Chocolate Chip Pudding

cal/serving 171   *Serves 8*

1 packet (100 gm) chocolate chip biscuits
some chocolate sauce (ready made)

VANILLA SPONGE CAKE
2 large eggs - separate yolk and white
5 tbsp powdered sugar
5 tbsp maida (plain flour)
1 tsp baking powder
1 tsp vanilla essence

CUSTARD SAUCE
½ kg (2½ cups) toned milk
3 tbsp custard powder
3 tbsp sugar
½ tsp vanilla essence

1. To prepare the cake, grease a loaf shaped cake tin. Sift maida with baking powder. Keep aside. In a clean, dry pan beat egg whites till stiff. Add sugar gradually, beating after each addition. When all the sugar has been used, add the egg yolks. Fold in the maida with a wooden spoon, moving the spoon upwards and then downwards (fold) to mix in the maida. When the maida is well mixed, transfer to the greased tin and bake at 200°C for 12-15 minutes. Remove from the oven after 5 minutes. Cut into thin fingers and keep aside.
2. To prepare the custard, dissolve the custard powder in a little milk. Boil the rest of the milk and add the custard paste when the milk boils. Cook on low heat till it turns slightly thick. Add sugar and cook for a few minutes till sugar dissolves. Remove from fire. Add essence.
3. Break all biscuits roughly, each biscuit into 6-8 pieces, (small pieces). Keep aside.
4. To assemble the dessert, in a medium size serving dish arrange a layer of sponge fingers. Soak them with some hot custard.
5. Sprinkle half the biscuits on it, to cover.
6. Again arrange a layer of sponge fingers.
7. Pour custard to cover completely. Chill. Sprinkle remaining biscuits.
8. Squeeze some chocolate sauce in a design over it, may be continuous diagonal lines, or in circles. Serve chilled.

Apple Meringue Pudding

Serves 10   *cal/serving* 96

6 apples - peeled and sliced thinly
3/4 teacup brown sugar
1 tbsp salted butter - melted
4-5 almonds - cut into thin long pieces

POWDER TOGETHER
3-4 laung (cloves)
½" stick dalchini (cinnamon)
¼ tsp grated jaiphal (nutmeg)

MERINGUE
2 egg whites
1/8 tsp salt
½ cup powdered sugar
1 tbsp grated lemon rind (from 2 lemons, preferably green)

1. Place thinly sliced apples in a baking dish.
2. Combine sugar, spices and melted butter in a small bowl.
3. Sprinkle sugar over the apples in the dish.
4. Bake at 200°C for 20 minutes or until apples are tender.
5. Remove from the oven. Cool the pudding.
6. To prepare the meringue, beat egg whites with an electric egg beater until fluffy.
7. Add salt and powdered sugar and beat more until stiff peaks form.
8. To get lemon rind, wash the lemons and grate them gently without grating the white pith beneath the peel. Fold the lemon rind into the beaten egg whites.
9. Spread meringue (egg whites) all over the apples. With a fork make small peaks in the meringue.
10. Sprinkle almonds. Bake at 200°C for 10 minutes or until golden brown. Serve warm.

Steamed Caramel Custard

cal/serving   150   *Serves 6*

3 tea cups milk
9 tsp sugar
3 tbsp milk powder
1 tsp vanilla custard powder
3 eggs
1 tsp vanilla essence

CARAMEL TOPPING
3 tsp sugar

1. Mix the milk with sugar, milk powder and custard powder. Mix well to dissolve all the lumps. Keep it on fire and boil stirring continuously. After the boil, reduce heat and simmer for 5 minutes. Remove from heat and cool.
2. Beat the eggs and vanilla essence well with an egg beater till light and fluffy.
3. Add the well beaten eggs to the cooled milk mixture. Keep aside.
4. Sprinkle 3 tsp of sugar at the bottom of a jelly mould. Place the mould over a slow flame holding it with a tongs and melt the sugar till the liquid turns golden brown. Remove from fire and spread it evenly over the base of the mould. Cool till the sugar is set at the bottom of the vessel.
5. Pour the milk-egg mixture in the mould. Cover well with aluminium foil and place a lid on top.
6. Pour 1½ cups water in a pressure cooker and place the covered mould in it. Pressure cook to give 4 whistles. Remove from heat. Let the pressure drop by itself.
7. Keep the pudding in the fridge so that it gets cold and sets well. Do not unmould till it turns cold.
8. To unmould at the time of serving, run a knife all around the mould and then invert it on a plate. Give a slight jerk to unmould the pudding. Decorate with fresh fruits and serve.

Note :   You may set the pudding in a ring mould (a mould with a hole in the centre) so that you can fill the centre with fresh fruits.

Queen Pudding

cal/serving   173   *Serves 6*

3 large eggs
6 heaped tbsp rusk crumbs
4 level tbsp sugar
1 tbsp desi ghee or margarine
1 level tsp baking powder
½ tsp vanilla essence
1 tbsp walnuts - broken into small pieces
1 tbsp kishmish - raisins
4-5 glace cherries - cut into thin rings
a small piece of lemon peel - cut into tiny bits - optional
1 cup hot milk

APPLE CUSTARD SAUCE
½ kg (2½ cups) milk
1 heaped tbsp custard powder
3 tbsp sugar
½ apple - cut into small pieces

1. Grease a round baking tin of 6"-7" diameter. Arrange lemon peels, walnuts, raisins & cherries in the tin so that they cover the base of the baking tin. Keep the baking tin aside.
2. Beat egg whites in a dry pan till stiff. Mix in egg yolks and beat again.
3. Add crumbs, sugar, ghee, baking powder and vanilla essence. Beat well to get a mixture of a thick **pouring** consistency.
4. Pour the mixture gently in the arranged greased tin, over the dry fruits.
5. Bake in a preheated oven for 25-30 minutes at 200°C.
6. When baked, remove from the tin to a serving dish.
7. Immediately pour 1 cup of hot boiling milk, all over the pudding, to make the pudding extra soft. Keep aside.
8. Prepare custard by dissolving custard powder in ½ cup of cold milk.
9. Heat 2 cups of milk with sugar. When it boils, add custard powder, stirring continuously. Add apple pieces. Cook for 2-3 minutes till it coats the spoon.
10. Serve the pudding cold in summers with chilled custard or at room temperature with very hot custard in winters.

Mango Cheese Cake

cal/serving   120   *Serves 6*   *Picture on page 1*

CRUST
10 Marie biscuits or digestive biscuits
1 tsp dried ginger powder (sonth)
2 tsp honey, 3 tsp milk

CREAM CHEESE (PANEER)
1 kg milk, 1 tsp citric acid crystals, ½ cup warm water

OTHER INGREDIENTS
1 cup fresh curd (prepared from skimmed milk) - hang for 15-20 minutes
1 large mango - chopped (1 cup)
1½ tsp gelatine
3 tbsp honey
1 slice of mango - cut into ¼" pieces
2 tbsp thin cream (optional)

TOPPING
1 mango - cut into neat squares or scooped to get balls
cherries - fresh or tinned, mint leaf, 1 tsp chocolate sauce(optional)

1. For the crust, crush biscuits with a rolling pin (belan) to get coarse biscuit crumbs.
2. Place the crushed biscuits in a bowl. Add dry ginger, honey and milk. Mix well. Press the mixture at the bottom of a small shallow dish. Cover and place the dish in the freezer compartment of the fridge for 15 minutes to set.
3. Hang the curd in a muslin cloth for 15-20 minutes. Squeeze to drain extra water to get about 1/3 cup thick curd.
4. To make the cream cheese, place the milk in heavy bottomed pan and bring to a boil. Remove from heat.
5. In another bowl mix citric acid and warm water.
6. Add citric acid mixture to the milk. Return to fire & boil for 3- 4 minutes, stirring till milk curdles well. Remove from fire & let it remain in water for few minutes.
7. Drain in a muslin cloth or a strainer. Sprinkle ½ cup chilled water on it to(this will keep the cream cheese soft).
8. Blend in a blender hung curd, chopped full mango and honey in a blender to a smooth puree. Remove the puree in a bowl.
9. Soak gelatine in ¼ cup water. Heat on low flame until dissolved.
10. Add dissolved gelatine, cream & pieces of 1 slice of mango to the pureed mangoes, mix. Pour it over the set biscuit crust. Place in the fridge to set for 2- 3 hours.
11. Decorate with choclate sauce(optional), mango balls, cherries and mint leaves.

Glazed Pineapple Pudding

Picture on facing page   *Serves 12*   *cal/serving*   132

SPONGE CAKE
4 large eggs
85 gms (1 tea cup) maida (plain flour), 1 tsp level baking powder
115 gms (1 tea cup) powdered sugar
1 tsp vanilla essence, 1 tsp pineapple essence, 1½ tbsp hot boiling water

OTHER INGREDIENTS
a tin of fruit cocktail or soft fresh fruits - cut fruit into tiny pieces (1 cup)
4 tsp gelatine, 4 tbsp water
2 tea cups milk, 1 tea cup sugar
1 tea cup curd - beaten, juice of 1½ lemons
1 tsp pineapple essence, few drops yellow colour

GLAZE
¼ cup strawberry jam, ¼ cup water, 2 tsp gelatine

1. To prepare a sponge cake, separate white and yellow of eggs. Beat egg whites till stiff. Add sugar gradually (2 tbsp at a time) and keep beating till all sugar is used.
2. Add yolks. Mix well. Add both the essences. Add boiling water, half tbsp at a time and beat more. Beat till the mixture of eggs and sugar is thick and frothy and is three times in volume.
3. Sift maida with baking powder. Fold in maida gently, using a spoon (not a beater) adding half of it at a time. Put in a greased and dusted tin 8-9" diameter (a big cake tin) and bake for 30-35 minutes in a preheated oven at 180°C. Remove from tin after the cake cools. Keep the sponge cake aside.
4. Sprinkle gelatine over water in a small pan. Heat on low flame to dissolve it. Keep aside. Mix sugar & milk and heat slightly to dissolve sugar. Remove from fire. Add gelatine solution to milk, stirring continuously. Let it cool down.
5. After it cools, stir in whipped curd & lemon juice. Add essence and colour. Chill.
6. Arrange the sponge cake in a serving platter or a full plate.
7. Soak with syrup of tinned fruit or with cold milk to make the cake moist. Touch with the hand to check that it feels moist. Spread fruits. Keep aside.
8. When the yogurt is slightly thick but not yet set, spoon over the fruits on the cake. Let it fall on the sides and cover the sides too. Chill in the freezer to set fast.
9. To prepare the glaze, dissolve gelatine in water. Keep on very low heat till it dissolves. Stir in the jam. Cook for 1-2 minutes on low heat. Remove from fire.
10. When the glaze is beginning to set, spoon it over the set yogurt. Arrange fruits on the glaze. Keep in the refrigerator and not in the freezer till serving time.

Glazed Pineapple Pudding; Juicy Fruit Jelly: Recipe on page 125 ➢

Chocolate Souffle

Serves 6   *cal/serving* 79

Cream has been substituted with yogurt to make a delicious souffle!

2 cups toned milk
2 tbsp cornflour
3 tbsp cocoa
9 tbsp sugar
½ tsp butter
2 tsp gelatine
3/4 cup thick curd (of toned milk) - hung for ½ hour and squeezed well
1½ tsp vanilla essence
fresh fruits and mint to garnish

1. Dissolve cornflour and cocoa in ½ cup warm milk.
2. Keep rest of the milk on fire. When it starts boiling, add the dissolved cornflour and cocoa, stirring continuously. Add the sugar also. Cook, stirring till the milk turns slightly thick, like custard and coats the spoon. Remove from fire. Mix in butter. Keep chocolate custard aside.
3. Sprinkle gelatine on ¼ cup water kept in a small pan. Keep on low flame till gelatine dissolves. Remove from fire and add to the chocolate custard.
4. Whip the hung curd till smooth. Put in a cup and add enough milk, (about ¼ cup milk) to make upto 3/4 cup. Add essence also.
5. Add the curd mix to the cooled chocolate custard and mix well. Transfer to a serving dish and keep in the fridge till set. Garnish with fruit & mint.

Apple Crumble

cal/serving   75   *Serves 4*

4 apples - cut into four, peeled and sliced thinly
3 tsp castor sugar
½ tsp cinnamon (dalchini) powder
1 tbsp custard powder
8 marie biscuits - crushed coarsely

1. Cook the apples with sugar, cinnamon powder, and ¼ cup of water over low heat in an open pan, for about 15 minutes, until excess liquid dries up. Leave to cool.
2. Mix together the marie biscuits and the custard powder with the apple mixture.
3. Transfer to an oven proof serving dish. Place in a hot oven at 200°C for 15 minutes.
4. Serve immediately accompanied with custard.

Light Chocolate Sandesh

cal/serving   88   *Serves 10*

1 kg toned (skimmed) milk, juice of 1 lemon
2 tbsp cocoa powder, 10 tbsp powdered sugar
¼ tsp chhoti illaichi (green cardamom) powder
a few almonds - cut into halves, for garnishing

1. Boil milk. Add lemon juice only after the milk boils. Stir till it curdles. Add a little more lemon juice if it does not curdle properly. See that the green water (whey) separates. Strain the chenna through a muslin cloth. Dip the chenna tied in the cloth in ice cold water for 10 minutes. Hang for 15 minutes or more to drain out the whey (liquid). Squeeze liquid, if any.
2. Put chenna, cocoa, sugar and cardamom powder in a mixer and blend till smooth. Remove from blender and transfer to a heavy bottomed kadhai.
3. Cook for 3-4 minutes till the chhenna turns dry and becomes thick.
4. Grease tiny biscuit moulds. Put an almond half, white side (cut) down.
5. Fill with mixture and press well. Invert on to a serving plate. Keep covered in the fridge till serving time.

Crunchy Bread Pudding

Serves 6   *cal/serving*   113

3-4 brown bread slices
½ cup orange or pineapple juice, ready made

CUSTARD
3 cups milk
3 tbsp custard powder dissolved in ½ cup cold milk
2½ - 3 tbsp sugar
1 banana
1 apple
½ cup halved grapes or any seasonal fruit

TOPPING
2 chocolate chip cookies - crushed coarsely

1. Cut the sides of bread and then cut each into 4 pieces and arrange at the bottom of the serving dish.
2. Soak with 5-6 tbsp of juice, such that the bread feels moist when touched.
3. To prepare the custard, heat 3 cups milk. When it boils, add the custard dissolved in ½ cup milk. Keep stirring continuously. Add sugar. Remove from fire after the custard turns thick and coats the back of the spoon nicely. Remove from fire and keep aside.
4. Spread bananas on the soaked bread. Then spread the apples and lastly the grapes on the bread.
5. Pour the hot custard over the fruits to cover completely. Chill.
6. At serving time, sprinkle the crushed cookies and serve immediately.

Fresh Peaches in Sauce

cal/serving 70   *Serves 8*

An interesting way of serving peaches. Microwaving the peaches makes it very simple.

4 big (ripe & firm) peaches (aadus)
6 tbsp sugar
2 cups water
1 tsp lemon juice

SAUCE
2 tbsp vanilla custard powder dissolved in ¼ cup water

GARNISHING
a few fresh grapes or cherries
or
some blanched almonds

1. Wash peaches well. Divide into two halves by running a knife all around at the centre. Twist the two sides in opposite directions and then pull the two parts apart to divide the peach into two equal halves. Remove the seed carefully.

2. To microwave the peaches, place them in a flat dish. Sprinkle sugar with a tbsp on all the peaches.

3. Pour water and lemon juice on the peaches.

4. Micro high for 5-6 minutes or till the peaches turn very soft, depending upon the ripeness of the fruit. Cool and remove the peel. The conventional way of stewing peaches is to boil 2 cups water with 6 tbsp sugar and lemon juice. Cover and cook the peaches in it for about 3-4 minutes till they turn soft but yet keep holding on to their shape.

5. Peel the peaches and arrange the stewed peaches in a clean serving dish which is not too high (1½"-2" height), leaving behind the sugar syrup. Keep aside.

6. Strain the sugar syrup. Dissolve custard powder in ¼ cup water and add to the sugar syrup.

7. Cook the sugar syrup, stirring continuously, till thick and translucent. Check sugar and add more if required.

8. Pour the ready sauce over the arranged peaches in the dish. Decorate the peaches by placing a fresh cherry or a grape in the centre of each piece. Serve chilled.

Orange Cake with Orange Sauce

Serves 15   *cal/serving   110*

Just 2 eggs are used to prepare a big cake, right for 15 people. The orange juice if fresh is naturally healthier, but ready made juice will also do!

1¾ cups maida (plain flour)
1½ tsp baking powder
1 cup orange juice
1/3 cup oil
1¼ cups powdered sugar
2 eggs
¼ tsp dalchini (cinnamon powder)
4-6 almonds - cut into fine pieces
1-2 tbsp brown sugar

SYRUP
½ cup orange juice, 3 tbsp honey
1 tbsp cornflour

1. To prepare the cake, sift maida with baking powder.
2. Beat eggs till stiff in a clean, dry pan.
3. Add sugar gradually and beat well till frothy.
4. Add oil, little at a time and keep beating.
5. Add orange juice and cinnamon powder.
6. Add ½ of the maida and mix gently. Add the left over maida too.
7. Transfer to a greased ring mould, (a jelly mould with a hole in the centre). Sprinkle brown sugar and almonds on top.
8. Bake at 180°C for 30-35 minutes. Bake till a knife inserted in it comes out clean. Cool and remove from dish. Keep aside.
9. Mix all ingredients of the syrup and cook till it attains a coating consistency.
10. Transfer the cake to a serving dish. Prick lightly. Pour the syrup over the cake. Serve.

Note: When you use ready made orange juice, 1 small pack of ready made orange juice (Tropicana) is enough for the cake and the sauce also. If you wish, you may make extra sauce and serve in a sauce boat along with the cake.

Juicy Fruit Jelly

Picture on page 118   *Serves 10*   *cal/serving 84*

2 packs (85 gm each) pineapple jelly
2 small packs (500 ml) pineapple juice
400 ml (2 cups) water

FRESH FRUITS
3/4 cup green grapes
3/4 cup black grapes
1 kiwi
1 apple - cut into small pieces
3-4 strawberries - cut into slices
1 orange - segments removed

CUSTARD SAUCE
½ kg (2½ cups) toned milk
3 tbsp custard powder
3 tbsp sugar
½ tsp vanilla essence

1. Boil water. Remove from fire. Sprinkle jelly on it. Leave it for 2 minutes. Mix well. Transfer from one pan to another to dissolve the jelly nicely.
2. Add the juice and mix well. Keep in the freezer to set.
3. When slightly set, beat well and mix in the fruits.
4. Spoon out in a serving dish. Keep covered in the refrigerator till serving time.
5. To prepare the custard, dissolve the custard powder in a little milk. Boil the rest of the milk and add the custard paste when the milk boils. Cook on low heat till it turns slightly thick. Add sugar and cook for a few minutes till sugar dissolves. Remove from fire. Add essence.
6. Serve fruit jelly with custard served in a separate sauce boat.

Apple & Date Pudding

Serves 6   *cal/serving*   102

a sponge cake, 1½ - 2" thick, about 7" diameter
½ cup cold milk
10-12 almonds - blanched and chopped, optional

APPLE LAYER
2 apples - peeled and grated
1 tsp lemon juice
3 tbsp sugar
¼ tsp dalchini (cinnamon) powder
¼ cup water

DATE SAUCE
100 gm (1 cup) dates
½ cup water
1 tsp cornflour - dissolved in ½ cup water

1. Cut sponge cake into half horizontally to get 2 pieces of the cake.
2. Place one piece in the serving dish. Soak with 4-5 tbsp of milk, such that the cake feels moist to touch. Place the other piece of cake in a plate and soak that piece too. Keep aside.
3. Peel and grate apples thickly. Put in a pan with lemon juice, sugar, cinnamon powder and ¼ cup water. Cook on medium flame for 5-7 minutes till almost dry, but do not dry them too much.
4. Spread a thick layer of cooked apples on the soaked cake.
5. Sprinkle half the almonds on top if you wish. Place the other piece of soaked cake on top and press gently. Keep aside.
6. To prepare the date sauce, wash and deseed dates and chop them finely. Boil chopped dates in ½ cup water for 4-5 minutes or till soft. Remove from fire and cool. Blend in a blender only for a few seconds so as not to mash the dates completely. Mix in 1 tsp cornflour with ½ cup water and add to the date puree. Cook the date sauce for 2-3 minutes after the boil, stirring continuously till slightly thick.
7. Pour the sauce over the cake such as to cover it completely on the top. Tilt the dish a little to cover the sides also.
8. To decorate, sprinkle some blanched (skin removed) and chopped almonds. Chill before serving.

Nita Mehta's BEST SELLERS

MUGHLAI Veg. Khaana

All Time Favourite SNACKS

CONTINENTAL Vegetarian

HANDI TAWA KADHAI

STAY SLIM...EAT RIGHT

PUNJABI COOKING

ITALIAN Non-Vegetarian

The Best of CHICKEN Recipes

CHINESE Non-Vegetarian

MICROWAVE Non Veg.

Chutneys, Squashes, Pickles

Flavours of INDIAN COOKING (All Colour)

MORE CHICKEN

Taste of KASHMIR

Taste of PUNJAB

Taste of RAJASTHAN

Delicious THAI Cookery

BREAKFAST Veg. Special

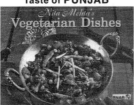
VEGETARIAN DISHES

LOW CALORIE Non Veg.

Still More PANEER

QUICK MEALS

SNACKS Non Veg.

SANDWICHES

PARTY FOOD

Nita Mehta's BEST SELLERS

CAKES & CHOCOLATES

Delicious ZERO OIL

ICE CREAM

DINNER MENUS from around the world

FOOD FOR CHILDREN

LOW CALORIE Recipes

LOW FAT Tasty Recipes

MOCKTAILS & SNACKS

PRESSURE COOKING

Soups Salads & Starters

SOUTH INDIAN

The Art of BAKING

MORE SNACKS

Favourite NON-VEGETARIAN

DAL & ROTI

BREAKFAST Non-Veg.

PASTA & CORN

JHATPAT KHAANA

Taste of GUJARAT

CHAAWAL

NAVRATRI RECIPES

GREEN VEGETABLES

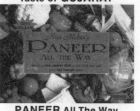

PANEER All The Way

MORE PANEER

CHINESE Cookery

MICROWAVE Cookery

DESSERTS & PUDDINGS

MORE DESSERTS